The Many Stories of Our Beloved Community

THE MANY STORIES OF OUR BELOVED COMMUNITY

Honoring Young Children's Kinship and Connections with the World

Rukia Monique Rogers

Redleaf Press®
www.redleafpress.org
800-423-8309

Published by Redleaf Press
10 Yorkton Court
St. Paul, MN 55117
www.redleafpress.org

First edition 2024
Cover design by Louise OFarrell
Cover photographs by Jessica Horsley and SJ Travel Footage / stock.adobe.com
Interior design by Louise OFarrell
Typeset in Adobe Chaparral Pro
Printed in the United States of America
31 30 29 28 27 26 25 24   1 2 3 4 5 6 7 8

Library of Congress Cataloging-in-Publication Data
Names: Rogers, Rukia Monique, author.
Title: The many stories of our beloved community : honoring young children's kinship and connections with the world / by Rukia Monique Rogers.
Description: First edition. | St. Paul, MN : Redleaf Press, [2024] | Includes index. | Summary: "Rukia Monique Rogers takes an inspiring look at the values, practices, and relationships of the Highlander School in Atlanta, Georgia, rooted in the vision of the beloved community as espoused by Reverend Dr. Martin Luther King Jr. Sharing abundant stories from the school, the book is an invitation to reflect on your own practices and to reimagine early childhood programs, believing in the full human potential for care, love, and justice and nurturing our connections with the Earth and each other"— Provided by publisher.
Identifiers: LCCN 2023045195 (print) | LCCN 2023045196 (ebook) | ISBN 9781605547732 (paperback) | ISBN 9781605547749 (ebook)
Subjects: LCSH: Early childhood education—Georgia—Atlanta. | Progressive education—Georgia—Atlanta. | Highlander School (Atlanta, Ga.)—History. | Day care centers—Activity programs—Georgia—Atlanta.
Classification: LCC LB1139.27.G4 R64 2024 (print) | LCC LB1139.27.G4 (ebook) | DDC 372.2109758/231—dc23/eng/20231017
LC record available at https://lccn.loc.gov/2023045195
LC ebook record available at https://lccn.loc.gov/2023045196

Printed on acid-free paper

To my dear mother, Beverly Ann Rogers. The vision of the Highlander School and her stories are the embodiment of my mother's living spirit, her generosity, activism, and deep connection with this earth. She was the magic of my childhood.

Contents

Acknowledgments

I would like to start by acknowledging my grandmother. She has been central in giving me the breath to do this work. You, Nana, are the center of telling these stories. Thank you for nurturing me during this time, laying hands upon me, oiling my scalp, pouring unconditional love upon me and our school and the children.

This book and the stories shared are the result of the love, work, and fierce commitment of my community to a reimagined world. It was written in the midst of tremendous growth, shifts in my internal thinking, and new understandings about my role as an educator and the role of schools our communities. The book captures who we are and our evolution, and I also recognize that it's an ongoing story with gaps of time and space.

I had the honor of compiling these stories, but it is a testament to the collective work of the children, educators, families, colleagues, and earth-centered practitioners. To all of you, I am indebted to your grace, care, and unwavering hard work. We loved, collaborated, disagreed, and found ways to create something new! This book specifically highlights the collaboration and work of Latisha Flowers and Estefhaney Lopez in their role as studio teachers, and fellow educators Akou Apedo, Jamilah Bilal, Daisey Dominguez, Jessica Horsley, Tori Jackson, Nicole Johnson, Nicole Olauson, and Bianca Stewart who nourished the most loving environments, capturing children's learning and sharing their own.

Our work and therefore this book has been deeply influenced by our colleagues—our community of early childhood educators, organizers, and activists. This includes the legacy of the activists of the Black Panther Movement the 1960s, rooted in collective responsibility with a commitment to meeting the needs of the community. I've been inspired by Angela Davis, who expanded my thinking not only to include anti-racism in my work but to progress toward a sustainable work. In addition, bell hooks provided inspiration with a pedagogy rooted in liberation and love, along with the intersection of environmental injustice. Inspiration also comes from the educators from Aotearoa New Zealand and Reggio Emilia, to name a few.

I would like to express my gratitude to the following colleagues: Ijumaa Jordan, I give thanks for your ongoing work and the way you center and at times challenge us in our anti-bias work. Your words and practice have been profoundly influential.

Sonya Shoptaugh, our sisterhood and your guidance has held and challenged me as a leader to think with creativity and act with courage. Your inquiry and guiding professional development have supported so many of the stories shared.

Linda Grant, I thank you for your years of mentoring and willingness to edit my endless writings and thoughtful collaboration.

I express my deepest gratitude to this land and earth which has held me, nourished my soul, and provided the canopy above my head and the strength beneath my feet, a source of tremendous energy, wisdom, and healing that has grounded my ability to see children's innate connections.

This gratitude is extended to the earth practitioners who helped create the threads between the school's values and lived practices. Your collaboration has been particularly essential for shifting our views about our relationship with this earth.

Much gratitude to:

Robby Astrove, our school's arborist and environmental educator. Your contribution and work with the school has helped create the context for the healing of the land, the process of re-matriation, and the children's love of trees. You've been our unwavering co-conspirator in this work.

Farmer T for helping us to actualize the children's idea of community garden to share with the world. You were generous with your time, inviting us to your farm and helping us rethink our understanding of farming and the power found in growing our own food.

Mekko Kernell Chebon, who called us in as a community to help save the Weelaunee Forest (an urban forest in Atlanta) and reminded us that the Muscogee people, unlike depicted in history books, are still alive and continuing to fight for this land, earth, and water. Your spiritual leadership and presence helped tell the stories of this land.

David Camacho for guiding our community in celebrating the Days of the Dead. Your wisdom and words help us to reclaim an honoring of the cycle of life.

I want to acknowledge the many children and families who have called the Highlander School home, with special acknowledgement to Sasha Von Hanna, who helped with so many edits. Each day, I've gotten to hear the hopes and dreams of families and listen and learn from children who remind me of the infinite possibles for us living in a harmonious way.

Thank you Redleaf Press editor Melissa York for your thoughtful guidance, rallying, and support.

Again and again, I return to acknowledging my mother, Beverly Ann Rogers.

She was a young mother when she made her way through the University of Wisconsin, wrestling with profound questions. I got to listen in and hear the tingles of revolutionary ideas. Madison, Wisconsin, and its surrounding lakes, land, and schools were the backdrop for my play and inquiry. I remember my mother picking me up from kindergarten to attend my first protest and telling me the importance of speaking up. My mother would forever challenge me to question the status quo and presumptions taught in school. She would go on to have a long career in the corporate world, but her spirituality and the earth called to her. An avid gardener, cook, seamstress, and healer, my mother had begun to study herbalism, massage therapy, and raw food, and had hopes of opening a spa before she passed. The school is full of her memories, her books of herbalism, her teapots, recipes for scrubs, and knowledge of the many ways in which this earth heals. Her spirit and love are like the waves of an ocean, powerful in constant motion, a driving force in my life.

1 Introduction

> *We will carry what we know—what it can mean to have your country under you like a hammock, what it is to take part in the world, instead of using your people as fodder in a war to control the world's meaning and expression. We will disrupt through witness, remembrance, and the courtship of the imagination. We will escort children past the darkest warrens of the forest. We will construct kites that stay aloft in the rain. We will champion what is beautiful.*
>
> —Barry Lopez, essayist and nature writer

What could it mean to have a community or country under you like a hammock?

This book is an invitation to reimagine early childhood education programs, and thus our world. Think of an earth-centered world full of human potential, care, love, and justice. Picture a beloved community where *every* being is honored for their sheer existence and has a village under them like a hammock. The beloved community is a powerful metaphor made widely known by Dr. Martin Luther King Jr. The beloved community for the Highlander School represents the possibilities for our ways of living together, a space that embodies a sense of belonging, equity, and community, where everyone's body and soul is nourished.

This book is the story of the journey of the Highlander School in Atlanta, Georgia, as we grew a beloved community, inspired by the instinctive connections, eagerness for relationships, and inherent knowledge of young children.

Our story starts with the recognition that the human family is beautifully intertwined with the natural world, which provides all the sustenance and life we need. Do we believe that the resources this earth has bestowed upon us, such as water and food, must be shared among the inhabitants in a manner that is equitable and just? If so, then one vital role of education is to support young children's innate connection and care for the natural world and to acquire ancient skills of respect and sustainability to protect and preserve this earth. Additionally, children strive to be woven into human connections. Their open and fluid way of being in the world invites us, as educators, to share this desire for connections and to support their construction of knowledge as people in relationship together.

Let me tell you the story of our school.

Rukia Rogers, Founder

As the founder of the Highlander School, I was inspired by my own upbringing, which had a fundamental impact on the lens through which I see the world and my approach to working with young children and families. I was born to a young and brilliant mom, and it was the nourishment and love from my community and village of aunts, uncles, grandparents, great-grandparents, and friends that not only ensured our survival but also helped us thrive. My mother became pregnant with me during her sophomore year of college. She was the first in our family to go to college, and she had a fierce determination to continue her education. So I was loved and held by many. It was a time and space of happiness, shared resources, and collective responsibility, where we played throughout the neighborhood for hours and we learned from our elders.

In the distance, the land and nature was my beloved community. My grandfather and his family were former sharecroppers who escaped the violence and terrorism of Jim Crow Mississippi to move to Milwaukee, Wisconsin. Even in this unfamiliar place they strived to maintain a connection to the land. It was my great-grandmother who showed me how to grow and harvest collard greens. My beloved community included Camp Sidney Cohen, a program designed to give Black and Brown children outdoor experiences, where I learned to canoe, camp, and vigorously engage with the natural world.

Because of my family experiences, as an early childhood educator I've carried with me an understanding that my relationship with each child is part of a greater interconnected village. This led to the vision I held as I endeavored to grow the Highlander School.

Our History, Our Vision

The conception of our school grew during a conversation in the summer of 2007, as I began discussing the boundless possibilities for early childhood education in the Atlanta metropolitan area with colleagues. I was deeply committed to creating a program that addressed the need for quality care and innovative approaches to early childhood education, while fostering children's awareness and respect for the environment and the natural world. The following are ideas that informed the vision we shared.

We are compelled to reimagine a world full of love, justice, and equity. We are inspired to fashion a community of learners, where children are viewed as "citizens of today." We envision a world where every child is able to dream and to reach his or her fullest potential.

We believe relationships are a framework for our lives together as well as our thinking and planning. We believe that knowledge is constructed in relationship with others, our community, our environment, and materials. Every encounter is an opportunity for an exchange of ideas and new perspectives.

Our name is inspired by our optimism that we can leave the world better than we found it. The Highlander School draws on the rich and vibrant culture of the southeast and honors the Highlander Folk School of Tennessee, founded in 1932 with the mission to educate and empower adults for social change. Students such as Rosa Parks, Dr. King, John Lewis, and others flocked to the school as it acted as a safe haven for dialogue and nonviolent resistance to social injustices. Our hope and illuminating dream is that the Highlander School will embody this same spirit of freedom and cultivate a community of learners who are thirsty for knowledge.

Part of this story has been reclaiming the values and connections that my ancestors once held. In the African worldview, as in many Indigenous communities including Native Americans, the land and the earth are imbued with spiritual energy that demands reverence and care. Land, plants, water, and animals cannot be owned by humans, as these entities have their own energy, feelings, and power. Although there is wide diversity within African and Indigenous cultures, this belief that Earth and all of its gifts are to be revered as divine is pervasive.

The Highlander School's Core Values

Our values bind us together and shape our world. The core values of the Highlander School guide our decision-making process regarding our curriculum, professional development, community interactions, and finances and spending.

The Rights of the Child

The child has a right to be seen as a competent and capable human being. We believe that children are born ready and eager to build loving relationships and to explore the world around them. We believe children have the right to be producers of their own knowledge instead of being drowned in predetermined and prefabricated educational standards. Children have the right to play as they choose, directed by their own free will.

Children have the right to receive support from thoughtful and reflective adults who scaffold and enhance their play experiences and continuously seek the children's perspectives. Children have the right to have their curious, eager minds and ideas taken seriously. We will treat children as today's citizens, not future ones. We commit ourselves to creating a culture that fosters children's self-esteem and dignity with love and respect.

The Rights of the Families

We believe that families have the right to be viewed as capable and devoted guardians of children. We believe that family partnerships are essential in creating a community of learners and constructing our school culture. Families have the right to be respected, to receive clear communications, to have personal privacy, and to be an integral part of the learning process. We will always seek and respect the points of view and perspectives of families.

The Rights of Educators and Staff

Educators have the right to be regarded as skilled, competent researchers and professionals who are eager for growth. We believe educators and staff have the right to receive fair wages for their work, to expect transparency, and to be an integral participant in the school's program. Staff have a right to the time, space, resources, and support to accomplish their work with young children.

Democracy and a Sense of Belonging

We believe that education has an essential role in a democratic society. We believe that every member of the community should feel empowered and have real opportunities to participate in the decision-making processes with a deep sense of belonging. This value is reflected in our traditions for welcoming new members of our community, the celebrations of their lives, and the integration of our collective home culture.

Equity and Social Justice

We believe that every human and thus every child is endowed with certain inalienable rights that include the right to attain their fullest potential through creative expression, thought, inquiry, collaboration, and dissension. It is our unwavering belief that education is a vehicle for citizens to realize those capabilities and create a more democratic, pluralistic, and just society.

In support of this belief, we feel strongly about providing an inclusive setting for children of all developmental abilities. Within the Reggio Emilia approach, children with special rights are prioritized in admissions. We believe that when children learn through shared experiences, it promotes a sense of belonging and sensitivity to one another. Additionally, children learn to value individual differences and how they contribute to the overall community.

We believe high-quality early childhood education and care is the gateway for equity and social justice and that having an experience in a progressive program as a young child is an indicator of later "success" or fulfillment. We believe that every child, family, and teacher has the right to equal opportunities to learning regardless of their learning style, gender, age, ability, race, ethnicity, or family background. We are committed to creating a quality program that is accessible to a diverse group

of children and families, incorporating anti-bias goals and supporting children to develop a strong self-identity while valuing the difference of others.

We hope that children will develop the passion to be creative thinkers, activists, and empathic citizens. You will find us celebrating heroes such as Dr. King and recognizing holidays that reflect a value of equity and social justice.

The Natural World and Conservation

We believe that a vital role of education is to connect young children to the natural world and to offer them the skills to serve as custodians for this earth. In a fast-paced world, our goal is to move slowly with great intention and help children connect to the rhythm of the natural world.

We delight and celebrate the change of seasons. You might find us studying the cycles of life and bringing the elements of the outdoors inside. We use natural and found materials, guiding children to care for their world through conservation, recycling, and reusing.

Our program emphasizes eliminating waste, using recycled and found materials, and utilizing products that do not harm the earth. We make these practices part of our learning approaches with young children, their families, and our community. This extends to our value of operating a school that is fiscally responsible and functions within our means through creativity and without sacrificing our core values.

Multiple Perspectives

We value multiple perspectives as this supports and challenges our own thinking and helps us to create new and deeper understandings. We avoid conformity but instead seek new and divergent voices. In that context, we celebrate intellectual freedom and creative conflict.

Transparency

We believe in making visible the thinking behind our planning and the hands-on work with young children and each other. We welcome discussions and questions about our planning, work, and documentation. Our desire is to create a program that is open to the community for collaboration with educators in early learning programs, colleges, and universities.

Joy

We value sheer happiness and delight! As a community, we cherish the richness of learning as it unfolds. We pay close attention to this process as we believe that we should be ruled not by the clock but by the natural rhythms of our bodies. We value our routines and see them as opportunities for meaningful learning. You'll find us deeply engaged in play, projects, and conversations for extended periods of time. We feel that this allows for complexity, as well as the joy of being.

Even in the joy, like many other early childhood programs we've struggled to align our practices with our core values. Without collective community support, how does one offer livable wages? The telling of our story is a reflection of the many questions and issues that early childhood educators have to navigate and wrestle with. As you read our story, I hope that you see your own identity as well as different perspectives.

About This Book

The book is organized to highlight our core values in action, giving time and thought to sharing with you how we spend our time and lives together.

2 Space and Time for Growing the Beloved Community

Cultivating the beloved community requires the intentional space and time to build our relationships, connections, and differing perspectives and to wrestle with the most profound questions. This chapter highlights the structures, including the organization of our days, seasons, and environments, that center our relationships and offer new ways (or remember old ways) to be in a community full of equity and care.

3 Honoring Rituals and Traditions

Listen to the unique ways in which we build community with children as an integral part of our rituals and traditions. Discover the ways that these unique moments of sharing and connections foster a sense of belonging and strengthen group identity. Consider the rituals and traditions you hold that uplift and generate camaraderie for your community.

4 Eagerness for Relationships

This chapter highlights our innate desire to be in relationship with the world and all that it encompasses. With this knowledge, we share the stories of the ways in which children strive for connection with all. Join us as we relish in studying children's competencies and skills in seeing other members of our community and their eagerness to be in relationship. Consider the ways you notice members of your community striving to be in relationship.

5 Playing, Learning, and Working Together

Hear our stories of children's natural approaches to playing, learning, and working together. Study how children recognize that they have shared ideas and interests and eagerly join together in collective pursuits. Take in stories of children joining together using dramatic play scripts, sensory/motor experiences, and repeated actions and patterns in their play. Delight in the many ways the Highlander School offers children opportunities to help others and make meaningful contributions to the community, strengthening bonds through shared joy and laughter. Consider how you might notice and enhance these shared connections in your own work with children.

6 Our Diverse Community and World

Our collection of stories in this chapter reflects children's attention and respect for our diverse community and world. The children 's appreciation for a diverse community and world is the embodiment of their profound ability to observe, notice, and be accepting of differences, using the fullness of their senses and bodies. Join us as we study children's points of view and competencies that offer educators more possibilities to navigate our work with them on behalf of countering bias. We introduce the anti-bias education goals as a framework we use with children for countering the dominant and pervasive messages of racism and other biases that contribute to inequity in our programs and the world.

7 Fighting for the Beloved Community

In this culminating chapter, we share the stories of how we support children to act on behalf of fairness for one another and their world. The stories show a strong image of children, with agency and citizenship, yearning to make a positive difference in the world and help forge a beloved community. The chapter is full of stories shedding light on how children make meaning of challenging issues of inequity and unfairness from a place of love, coupled with their courage to take action. The chapter challenges you to think about how your program can tackle unfairness in your community and the world.

This book is an expression of love and an invitation to reimagine the world and early childhood programs, upholding a belief in the full human potential for care, love, and justice, with children as our co-conspirators. We hope you will join us on this important journey.

2 Space and Time for Growing the Beloved Community

Children, language, lands: almost everything was stripped away, stolen when you weren't looking because you were trying to stay alive. In the face of such loss, one thing our people could not surrender was the meaning of land. In the settler mind, land was property, real estate, capital, or natural resources. But to our people, it was everything: identity, the connection to our ancestors, the home of our nonhuman kinfolk, our pharmacy, our library, the source of all that sustained us. Our lands were where our responsibility to the world was enacted, sacred ground. It belonged to itself; it was a gift, not a commodity, so it could never be bought or sold. These are the meanings people took with them when they were forced from their ancient homelands to new places.

—Robin Wall Kimmerer, *Braiding Sweetgrass*

We acknowledge that the Highlander School resides on the ancestral land of the Muscogee (Creek) people.

On this land Muscogee children played, Muscogee families loved, and Muscogee culture thrived. This land bore witness to their genocide, forced assimilation, and forced removal. We honor the First Persons of this land. We honor the Muscogee People, those who were here before us and those who remain with us.

We acknowledge that this land felt the presence of Africans as explorers, traders, and contributors to the culture of Turtle Island (also known as North America). This land is also a place where enslaved Africans lived, loved, survived, and thrived despite and in resistance to the physical and emotional trauma of enslavement. This land also witnessed and felt the presence of the hands, bodies, songs, stories, and culture that the African community brought with them, including their collective knowledge of the land.

Here I stand, here we stand . . . the embodiment of the joy and hopes and longings of our ancestors. Our very presence is resistance.

The Highlander School community commits itself to truth education, sharing the history and the legacy of colonization. Our approach to being in community and learning together includes reclaiming African and Indigenous values and culture harmed from colonization and genocide. In the process of reclaiming practices, traditions, and rituals, we create a synergy of peace and harmony within ourselves and the land. We seek a community that holds this earth, our interconnections and kinship with her, as central to our work.

Our rich curriculum encompasses our relationships and work with this land. This includes our planning, design of our environments, routines, selection of materials, and interactions. The curriculum emerges and uniquely derives from the identities of the land upon which we sit; our community; the interests of the children, educators, and families; and our values that embody who we are. Our hope is to create a community of inquiry, where children and educators alike are empowered to wonder together and pursue their curiosities. Grounded in our relationships, our curriculum connects active listening, thought-provoking exchanges, and documentation to give visibility to this process. In this process, the learner

is passionately engaged in acquiring their education by researching problems, collecting data with their senses, proposing theories, and creating new meaning. Far from a prescribed curriculum, we are most interested in fostering a community that is delighted by curiosity. What is it that children want to learn? What is it that we want to learn with them? Active listening also includes collaboration among the adults to make meaning of their observations and plan for next steps.

Our approach to learning has been deeply influenced by bell hooks, Marian Wright Edelman, Bettina Love, John Dewey, Lev Vygotsky, Dr. Martin Luther King Jr., and the educators of Reggio Emilia, Italy, among many others. Their work and thinking have helped shape our fundamental belief that learning is an active and social process. It is a cultural practice that connects individuals to their society and culture. In essence, we as humans are interconnected, and our knowledge, traditions, identity, and values are socially constructed. Therefore, we see the child not only as an individual but in the context of their relationships and encounters with the land, the world, their family, and the greater community, as well as the hopes and dreams of their ancestors.

Our Image of the Child

In designing the Highlander School, we commit ourselves to a strong image of the child. We believe that children and their voices are interconnected with this earth and our community; that the child is born with multiple ways of knowing, intuitions, and connections; and that the child is capable, intelligent, and full of complexity, wonder, and a desire to connect with others and the world around them. We see children as having a depth of existing knowledge that they bring to learning opportunities and believe that they have the right to be treated with respect and dignity and be a part of the decision-making process. Children are viewed not as passive participants but as active discoverers and constructors of their own knowledge. We resist the image of the child as a future worker or consumer, to be filled with predetermined knowledge. Instead, we recognize children as citizens of the world today and know that their sheer presence on this earth should be honored. Children are the greatest links to our ancestors, links between the past and present.

The Reggio Emilia educators believe that children have a Hundred Languages to express their realizations about the world. In our environment, we strive to invite exploration of those languages of learning by introducing children to a variety of materials and experiences that give them new perspectives regarding the world around them. We recognize and honor their symbolic representations of theories that can be expressed and valued through dramatic play, drawings, collage, clay creations, storytelling, music, recycled materials, paint, blocks, sand, and water, to name a few. In our setting children are provided with materials to explore and manipulate during play. These materials are necessary for the children to express their ideas and construct new knowledge. The environment invites the use of all the "languages" of communication and yet still provides opportunities for the children to explore interests and discuss ideas in small groups.

Because we hold a strong image of the child, the Highlander School is intentional in the design of our curriculum, and we create the space and time needed to engage in deep listening, calling upon the earth and the voices of children. In this way, we hope to ensure that children and adults dive deeply into the possibilities for creating a beloved community and a more compassionate, equitable world.

Places for Relationships

Every person needs a place that is furnished with hope.

—Widely attributed to poet and activist Maya Angelou

The environment is the most tangible and visible embodiment of the shared beliefs, values, and assumptions a community holds. We ask:

Can we hear the children's voices in our space? Do we see the hopes and dreams of our community?

Public school began at the turn of the century when business complained that workers didn't have basic skills. Our first schools were modeled after factories, and the institutionalization of school continues. As architect Frank Locker writes, "In the US, many of the same people who designed prisons also designed schools. What comes to mind when you see a long hall of closed doors, [a hall] that you can't be in without permission, and a bell that tells you when to come in, when to leave, when class starts, when it ends? What does that look like to you?"

In holding a strong image of the child, we resist. Young children have been raised in the love, warmth, and comfort of small families and communities for centuries and deserve that nurturing start to life. At the Highlander School we are imagining what a school could look like with a different vision. We've designed our spaces for relationships, filled with places to marvel and delight, with color, light, texture, and reflections of the identity of all of us. We want children to find ways to see one another, their identity and that of their ancestors, and grow relationships in our spaces. We value their perspectives as we intentionally plan spaces that invite these relationships.

The Highlander School resides in a blue craftsman bungalow built in 1945. We are located in the East Atlanta Village, a vibrant, eclectic community of older Black residents, transplants, families, artists, growers, musicians, and folks without homes. We are a community experiencing the culture shifts of gentrification and all the harm that comes in that process. Our neighborhood has lost many of its Black families and is less socioeconomically diverse than it used to be. We sit next to the crossroads of the city, next to major highways, a commercial district, and a residential community on McPherson Avenue, which is the resting place for General McPherson, a union general who passed away during the Civil War's Battle of Atlanta. The East Atlanta Village or EAV is mere miles from the birth and the final resting place of Dr. King. We are profoundly influenced by the energy of where we reside . . . its history, space, and time.

Follow on a tour of our community.

Windows

Our space is designed to foster connections among our whole community, humans and nonhumans. The Highlander School is intentionally designed with many windows so children can see each other and engage throughout the day. The children spend a lot of time peering through the windows into our community space, which we call the *parlor* in honor of our Southern cultural traditions. The children can also see into all of the classrooms from the side porches and into the baby room from the front porch, the gate, and the toddler classroom. All of the rooms have a view of our playscape and the natural world. The large windows and transparent doors create opportunities to be seen, see, and engage in conversations of the body and soul, with all of our community.

These photos illuminate the ongoing interactions that take place at the windows. Several children gravitate to each side of the window with curiosity. We try to imagine the children's perspectives as we observe them.

Are they drawn to the window because they recognize one another? See themselves? Are they attracted by the interesting reflections of light and shadow? Do they enjoy standing as they support themselves? What are they watching? Are they studying each other's faces and expressions?

What are they seeking as they mirror each other's hands? Are they trying to understand other people and practicing engagement skills? As they talk, wave, smile, knock, and giggle, it seems evident that they are most captivated with one another, with simple, pure joy.

Living Rooms

We refer to the children's primary classrooms as the "living rooms" because they are the spaces where we eat, sleep, gather, and live together. They are the spaces that hold the unique identity of each child and their families, where their personal items live. The living rooms also include spaces for dramatic play, construction, exploring visual mediums, and music. They are fluid spaces, open to change as they respond to emerging questions and interests. We also make sure that each of our living rooms is open to children and adults from other rooms to gather.

Each living room has a studio space. Inspired by the educators from Reggio Emilia, we believe that children have a right to expression and access to materials that facilitate their communication of ideas. Our teachers have created spaces of inquiry, which include visual mediums such as markers, drawing pens, paint, clay, natural collections, and more materials for children to explore and use for representing their thinking.

The Outdoor Porches

Our porches embody our rich culture. They are extensions of our living rooms, places to gather, converse, sing, play, and greet our neighbors. The porches hold furniture for sitting, tables, and found and natural materials that create conversations and meaningful exchanges with the whole community. They are also places of connection where children and adults from different living rooms converge in community together.

The Parlor

Our parlor, in the tradition of our culture, is a place to welcome guests, sit in comfort, and learn about the culture and identity of our school. It is also a fluid place used for digital landscapes, which utilizes technology and materials to re-create the embodiment of a scene or landscape. It is also a place for celebrating birthdays, a place of warmth and texture for gathering.

Everywhere, we display documentation through which one can hear the words, voices, and thinking of the children, educators, and families. It takes the form of cherished artifacts, collections of children's work, the community's shared ideas and questions, and reminders of rituals and the ways we live together.

Learning Encounters
Monday
Tuesday
Wednesday
Thursday

The Playscape

Our beloved playscape is designed to create a sense of place and reflect the identity of Georgia. These sentiments were inspired by my visits to New Zealand, where the environments reflect a deep connection that the Māori culture feels between the land and the people's identity and community. Each area on the playscape reflects aspects of Georgia's landmarks and native plants, including small hills to reflect that we live in a piedmont and a large beach house, surrounded by sand and coastal vegetation, to reflect Georgia's coast. There is a small river to reflect our local river, the Chattahoochee, and a garden and orchard that honors Georgian agriculture. It is a wild and beautiful space full of herbs, grass, squirrels, birds, bugs, and open-ended materials that support creativity and the birth of new ideas. It is a place of rematriation and the reclaiming of our kinship with this earth and our ancient practices.

Our front yard is home to our medicinal garden, where we are surrounded by lush blackberry and raspberry bushes and muscadines. The front yard is also the home of our community garden, designed in collaboration with the children, which is shared with all, including the more-than-human world.

Time for Relationships

We yearn to move with the rhythms of our bodies and natural world. In our fast-paced society, driven by capitalism and standardized productivity, we imagine and claim a way of being that allows time to savor our relationships. We are intentionally a small program with four living rooms of children from infants to five years of age, and all children may regularly move throughout our community with caregivers and teachers. You will find us celebrating each birthday, seasonal change, and solstice as a whole school community. There is plenty of time to laugh, play, eat, and joyfully engage with one another. With this gift of time, we find new ways of listening, not only to the human world but also to the calling of the land and this earth. The time and space that we hold allows us to experience layers of perspectives and delight in the wonders around us.

Questions for Reflection

What speaks to your soul about the Highlander School's environments and the ideas behind them? What challenges come up for you?

As you consider your own environment, can you identify places for relationships that you have planned or that naturally invite the children's connections? Where do you see materials that authentically honor the voices of the families?

What changes might you make to your own environment to invite relationships?

The Culture of Learning as a Community

Professional development unfolds every day as we create a culture of inquiry, curiosities, and wonderment in keeping with our understanding of the rights of educators. We hold that theorists, overwhelmingly white men, do not dictate our practices. Instead we use connections, listening, and collaboration to make meaning together, which helps us deepen our understandings for our profession. We plan professional development days as another space and time for us to reflect together, especially as it relates to our core values and practices. We also create opportunities to meet with colleagues from outside of our school to challenge and deepen our ideas and assumptions.

Educators spend an enormous amount of time listening to the perspectives of children. They observe, write notes, take photographs, and make recordings that we study together to make meaning. During our yearly retreats we have the space and time to focus on fostering staff relationships with one another and with nature, while we reflect on the documentation we have collected. Our reflections and new understandings aid us in fashioning a Declaration of Intent that outlines an area of study for the upcoming school year or longer. This Declaration of Intent is generated by staff at our yearly retreat, based on our values, ongoing observations of the children, and questions. The Declaration of Intent generates solidarity among the community and becomes a vital thread for collaboration, learning together, and sustained professional development. Here is an excerpt of our Declaration of Intent for the 2021–2022 school year. As you read through, you will notice how this document created the framework for our inquiry and professional development.

Declaration of Intent for Supporting Children's Eagerness for Relationships

The Highlander School Declaration of Intent
Rooted in Activism: Children, the Natural World, and Food Equity
2021–2022

We are beautifully intertwined with the natural world, which provides us with all the sustenance and life that we need. We believe that the resources that this earth has bestowed upon us, such as water and food, must be shared amongst the inhabitants in a manner that is equitable and just. Therefore, we believe that one vital role of education is to support young children's innate connection to the natural world and to acquire ancient skills to protect and preserve this earth.

Unfortunately, in a fast-paced and capitalistic-driven world, we often disrupt young children's affection for the natural world. Our goal is to move slowly with great intention and embrace the rhythms of this earth. We delight and celebrate the change of seasons, the cycles of life, and the wonders of our beloved world.

Before progress can be made on social issues like gender inequality and racism, work needs to be done to ensure the planet is sustainable enough for humans to even exist.

—Black political activist Angela Davis

The following is some of what we've collectively noticed and documented about the children's connection to and analysis of the natural world, the stories and evidence we considered in shaping our Declaration of Intent. With their whole spiritual bodies, children observe, study, and appreciate the aesthetics and phenomena of nature, whether in the patterns of a leaf, the sounds of the winds, or the movement of an insect. They communicate through the languages of drawings, mark making, storytelling, and oral expression. Their sense of community comes through as they include both humans and nonhumans alike, knowing that animals and all living creations hold citizenship in our world.

While discussing and creating representations of "what citizenship means" the children stated:

Violet: Living creatures are citizens.

Harper: I'm making some bears that are citizens.

Ellie: Citizens are not all the same. They look different but some are the same.

Aria: Babies are citizens.

Jalle: I'm drawing turtles that have tails. That's the momma turtle and that's the baby.

The children also informed us that they consider plants to be active members of our community. During a community project, the children chose members of our community to interview and create their portraits. Aside from interviewing the librarian, a firefighter, and other humans, they insisted on interviewing a tree, located in the front of a neighbor's house, that they had developed a relationship with over the year. They referred to the tree as the "Stoney Age Queen Leaf Tree." The following is an excerpt from their interview with the Stoney Age Queen Leaf Tree.

Nalu: Why are you so biiiigggg?!

Ms. Bianca: What did it say?

Nalu: It said because I have a lot of roots.

Langston: Why do you have a lot of branches?

Annie: Why do you have all this moss on you? It said because they put it here.

Ms. Estefhaney: How is it listening to us?

Nalu: I don't know what you're saying tree, I don't understand tree. Look at the trees arms, all the way up there.

Likewise, the children's sense of justice and equity is expansive. A dominant and recurring thread of their thinking over the last couple of years is the notion that food from our garden (and in general) should be shared. As Caroline put it, "We've been sharing our garden with the caterpillar, that's love." They've expressed that the food should be shared with all members of our community, especially those experiencing homelessness.

In upholding this beautiful and powerful image of children, we are eager to learn with and learn from them as they challenge our thinking about the natural world and food equity. We want to continue to create a culture in which children are empowered to have agency in this world now.

We declare our commitment to do research:

- How do children view the rights of the natural world?
- What can we learn from children about how they connect with, perceive, and relate to the natural world?
- How do children view food equity?
- What strategies and methods can we develop and use to hear the voices of the children as they explore the rights of the natural world?
- How do we support and cultivate children's ability to engage in activism as it relates to environmental justice, food justice, and so on?
- How do we hear the children's voices?

We will incorporate a variety of strategies to hear the children's voices, including listening to the children's expressions through the many languages of drawing, compositions, clay, and other visual comments and reflections, as well as observing their gestures and body language to better understand their perspectives of the natural world and our playscape.

We will use various tools to aid in our observations, including recording with writing tools and paper, photography, and video recording to document children's views of the natural world.

We will create a context to hear the children's voices through technology and digital landscapes and bring elements of the natural world inside.

We will create a cyclical process of listening, observing, documenting, interpreting, and revisiting previous experiences with children for clarification and new understandings of nature and its role in the children's lives.

Here are some elements of the projects we launched around our Declaration of Intent focused on the natural world and food equity. In collaboration with a variety of experts in environmental education, we enhanced our environments and playscape with plants native to Georgia to create more opportunities for children to build a relationship with the natural world. We learned together through farm visits with the children as well as through professional development, inviting growers to share with us the rituals of caring for our land and the plants on it. As part of educators' growth and learning, we read and discussed *Farming While Black* by Leah Penniman.

In collaboration with our community, including the children, families, gardeners, and environmental educators, we resolved to establish a community garden on behalf of the whole community and especially for those experiencing food insecurity. In chapter 7 you can read the detailed story of our activism on behalf of creating a community garden that ensued from our Declaration of Intent.

Dialogues with Families

In our beloved community, families are our partners. This partnership requires us to create the space and time to play, explore, and engage in dialogue. Educators lead a quarterly room meeting with families to build relationships as we explore materials and ask and answer questions for the whole school community. These explorations and conversations are parallel to what the children and educators are exploring day by day. Rooted in our relationships, we engage in brave and challenging conversations that reflect our community and the world's hopes, passions, and inequalities.

This particular year, we wanted to have a greater understanding of how children perceived community as well as to pay close attention to the language of mark making and drawing as a means of hearing someone's thinking and perspective. We invited families to explore with us. After

much playing with the materials, we asked them to create a representation of their view of community.

Each family holds a unique identity and history that they carry with them to the Highlander School. Just as a trunk relates to a tree, our families are part of us. They are crucial partners in our work. We do not view families as simply paying customers for whom we provide a service in exchange for cash. How does one commoditize love and care? Where children would have once been raised in a close-knit family or tribe, now we as early childhood educators partner with families in raising their children. It is through shared values, connections, love, and a culture of reciprocity that we build community. Each educator comes from a family too, and they are part of our community as well.

Our time together begins with a family tour during which our core values, history, documentation, and space are shared. Families are deciding whether our school is a good fit, and so are we. Upon enrollment, we conduct a home visit to meet with the family and learn their home culture; educators also share themselves.

We create many other opportunities to grow connections between home and school and to exchange ideas, including quarterly room meetings, conferences, and committee meetings. Ideally, families spend some time helping in the classroom, for example, documenting children's work, assisting with special projects, or having lunch with their child and community. With all elements of the child's world working together, we build an exciting yet nurturing environment to enhance their journey of learning and growth.

The following are some examples of how we communicate with families to uphold our partnership in raising children together.

- Home Visits: Home visits are conducted before enrollment to build relationships and learn about the identity of the family and educators.
- Bright Wheel App: Families and educators use this app to communicate, including signing in; sending messages; posting the times of feedings, diapering, and naps for younger children; and sharing photos.
- Daily Diaries: Educators generate daily stories featuring one or more children that highlight the learning process along with our questions. These stories are emailed to families to invite dialogue, posted on our documentation board, and archived in the room.
- Quarterly Room Meetings: Educators organize this time to share documentation and ongoing work, explore materials, exchange ideas, and build relationships.
- Individual Journal: Each child has their own journal that highlights their story, interests, relationships, and learning process and includes work samples and other documentation.
- Parent/Family Conferences: Individual family meetings are conducted twice a year. Educators share the child's journal and discuss their learning within the community, as well as the families' hopes and dreams for their child.
- Parent Council: The Parent Council consists of two representatives from each room. They support the school's overall communication with individual rooms, offer advice, and help to plan school events such as Teacher Appreciation Week and seasonal celebrations.
- Social Justice Committee: The Social Justice Committee supports the school's reflective practices and its connections with anti-bias goals.

Reimagining our world requires the space and time to live together with love and care. The social and emotional environment lays the foundation for all other work to unfold and take shape. We yearn for children and our community to not only survive but thrive from nourishment and, in turn, walk in the world from a place of confidence and self-worth, with the ability to show up for others and their beloved community.

3 Honoring Rituals and Traditions

Walking, I am listening to a deeper way. Suddenly all of my ancestors are behind me. Be still they say. Watch and listen. You are the result of the love of thousands.

—Linda Hogan, Chickasaw author

Children enter this world not as individuals but as the hopes and dreams of their families, communities, and ancestors. The essence of who we are is an embodiment of the spirits, of the traditions, and of the "love of thousands" that stood before us and with us. Children, young humans, are born with innate understandings, intuitions, and connections to this earth, our natural world, and beings both past and present. But the culture of school often struggles or fails to see the whole child. At the Highlander School we want to consider myriad possibilities for knowing children, teachers, families, and communities full well.

In our society's dominant approach to early childhood education, we often view the child through a lens of white American values that centers the child as an individual, a blank slate to be filled with information. We believe that this common approach and the term *child-centered* are steeped in the Western culture of individualism, consumption, and capitalism. This cultural view of the child is often deficit based and fails to recognize children's innate capabilities and desires for deep connections with others. Instead, the Highlander School places importance on centering relationships rather than individual children.

Family, community, and culture are fundamental to developing a strong identity as children come to understand where and how they belong and how they can contribute to the world. It is in this nurturing community that knowledge is constructed and traditions and ways of being are shared. Centering children as individuals and viewing the nuclear family as having sole responsibility for children's lives does not help us live in more nourishing ways of being together.

Questions for Reflection

What is your response to the quote at the beginning of this chapter?

How might the idea of children being the "result of the love of thousands" influence the work of early childhood programs?

At the Highlander School, we regularly ask ourselves:

- How do we welcome new members to our family/community?
- How does our community express our notions of love and affection?
- How do our celebrations of life, birth, rebirth, and death contribute to a collective sense of belonging that we can share with one another?

Consider a story of our ongoing journey to understand how we are thinking beyond child-centered practices and trying to live into a vision of the more expansive bonds we can foster.

Our First Los Días de los Muertos Celebration

As a new school we had not fully determined what our cultural practices would be. May 5 was fast approaching, and a parent suggested that we celebrate Cinco de Mayo. We were hesitant because we were well aware that such celebrations can be ripe with stereotypes and misunderstandings. However, we were confident in our need to gain a new perspective and learn, so we approached a parent of Mexican descent, David Comanche, for guidance. Even as a new school we had already determined that reaching out to hear voices from our community was central to our practices.

David was excited about the engagement, and he informed us that Cinco de Mayo was only a small celebration in a particular region of Mexico. Instead, he invited us to learn about and celebrate Los Días de los Muertos, or the Days of the Dead, the following autumn. David is a skillful storyteller and vividly shared the history of Los Días de los Muertos with the whole community. He crafted a letter that captured the essence of the Days of the Dead.

David Comanche's Letter to the Community

What are the Days of the Dead?

Los Días de los Muertos or the Days of the Dead, celebrated on November 1 and November 2, have their roots in the ancient societies of the Americas. This tradition survived the Spanish Conquest and adapted to the Catholicism brought over by the Spaniards. Like the Celtic traditions that center around fall harvests, Los Días de los Muertos resisted the desires of the Roman Catholic Church to be replaced with All Saints' Day and All Souls' Day. Instead of becoming days of serious prayer, reflecting a deep melancholic association with death, Los Días de los Muertos have retained a great deal of their roots and are still joyous days to remember and honor deceased loved ones. There are no witches and goblins or spooky spirits that go bump in the night. Instead, the two days are bright, colorful, festive, and filled with the vigor of life.

In Mexico, citizens visit cemeteries, where they spend the days decorating the graves of loved ones and prepare for the return of the departed spirits. Throughout the Southwest United States and in places with large Mexican populations, altars are built and surrounded with flowers, food, photos, and memorabilia associated with pursuits enjoyed by the deceased.

Día de los Inocentes (Day of the Innocents) is celebrated on November 1. On this day, deceased infants and children are honored and invited back to continue their part in the community of the living. White flowers and fragrant plants decorate their altars along with toys and piñatas. Activities associated with children's celebrations complete the atmosphere and welcome the spirit of the departed back on this festive occasion.

On November 2, Día de los Muertos is observed. As on the previous day, altars are constructed. They are adorned with orange marigolds, papel picado (paper cutouts), sugar skulls, and bread baked for the occasion (known as pan de muerto, "bread of the dead").

Unlike much of Western culture, the Indigenous peoples of the Americas embrace the role of death in the cycle of life, death, and rebirth. Death is embraced so the fear it holds on to the living is lessened and the beauty of life can be further appreciated. The great Mexican poet and Nobel Prize laureate Octavio Paz once wrote, "The Mexican is familiar with death, jokes about it, caresses it, sleeps with it, and celebrates it. It is one of his favorite playthings and his steadfast love."

Sincerely,

David

Death is difficult to deal with for many people. Los Días de los Muertos is a time to pause, reflect, and give thanks as a member of a community. The celebration offers a perfect metaphor to help young children, especially those recently affected by the passing of a loved one, to evolve their understanding of life and death as they grow, mature, and heal. This most natural of processes affects us all and will continue to do so for as long as we are a part of the living community, as well as a community that includes the departed.

Because we believe that children feel a never-ending resolve to understand the richness and complexities of life, we strive to create a community that reflects the unique identity of all our members. David's information about the Days of the Dead fortified our courage to celebrate the lives of our dearly departed. We asked ourselves:

- How would the children approach the subject of death? Would fear emerge?
- Would the process create a connection with the lives of children's relatives and their heritage?
- How would this celebration help all of us grow together as a community?
- Would this experience uncover the children's natural dispositions to be in communion with the larger mysteries of life?

The days leading up to the Days of the Dead were festive, as we filled the altar with marigolds, fruit, and colorful decor. Incense scented our hallways while we collectively prepared delicious smelling tamales—soon to become a mainstay on our lunch menu. The celebration began simply, as families were invited to bring photos of their "dearly departed" and items they had loved. The presence of these photographs and objects in our environment sparked heartfelt responses and conversations. The celebration was provocative for many members of our community, and understandably so. In our dominant culture we do not usually talk about matters of discomfort, and we rarely speak about death. Yet here was a gift of time and knowledge, calling on Indigenous values as we joined together to reclaim a different narrative about our shared lives.

The children were intuitively connected with their ancestors as they entered the room, bringing the framed images and stories their families had created. The children held the photos of their ancestors who had "gone back to nature" with extraordinary familiarity and sacredness. The teachers invited the children to draw their images, and as they drew, the stories unfolded.

August, who recently lost her beloved Aunt Brit, her mother's twin sister, held the picture tightly and then studied her face. "I want to make stars for her eyes," she said.

Sadie held up a picture of her Bubbie and pointed out how her Bubbie was holding her and her twin sister, Grace, as infants. With a warm smile, she said, "Bubbie is sad because she misses me."

At the same time, Porter looked fondly at a photo of his dog, Canyon, who had recently died. Her passing had generated emotions of sadness for Porter. He began to draw Canyon's picture and said, "I'm going to draw a heart cuz I love her."

Ian tightly held the framed picture of his grandfather, staring into his eyes. Ian is a mirror image of his grandfather, reflecting the shape of his face, nose, and eyes. His mother shared that her father died when she was young and she had never discussed his story with Ian. And yet there was a strong connection between Ian and his grandfather. He carried his picture with him most of the day and placed it next to his mat during naptime.

Vivian's face was tilted downward, and her tone was soft and low as she shared about her granddaddy. She said, "Granddaddy died. Grandmommy was my Grandmommy, then she died. She was my mom's mom." There was a small moment of silence, then Vivian said, "I miss my Grandaddy. We used to have a tray. It was a black tray. He made pickles for my mommy. We used to go to the park a lot of times."

Ilah approached Ms. Rukia's picture as Ms. Rukia shared her mother's story. Ilah listened compassionately and then began to draw a picture. She handed the drawing to Ms. Rukia and said, "These are your mother's tears . . . she misses you."

The children were eager to share their photographs and stories. They showed emotional wisdom, offering their ideas about what the dearly departed were experiencing and feeling. With great curiosity and our hearts overflowing, we listened as they navigated through the seriousness of death and the joy of honoring the lives of their dearly departed. The children's tender offerings touched us all deeply.

Celebrating Los Días de los Muertos or the Days of the Dead has been a transcendent experience for the entire school community. It has helped us reimagine the connections between the world of the living and those who, as the children say, have gone back to nature.

We are humbly grateful for David Comanche's leadership during our first celebration and the many we have had since then. His lessons embody the importance of finding joy as we appreciate the fullness of the life cycle. We continue to celebrate Los Días de los Muertos to this day, and it has become an integral part of the culture of our school and our identity and a celebration of our community.

Our Days of the Dead celebrations have also influenced how we reflect on and construct many of our curriculum and cultural practices. We don't just celebrate the Days of the Dead to honor cultural diversity. Instead we have been inspired to adopt the values embedded in this celebration because we see how it strengthens our connections with one another as partners in the larger meaning of life. We are committed to continuously offering children, families, and staff not just a window but a passageway to different ways of being together in the world.

Questions for Reflection

What is your response to this story of the celebration and values that the Highlander School is drawing on to create meaningful community bonds?

What wisdom and competencies did you hear in the children's perspectives about their ancestors?

What memories of your ancestors touch you in meaningful ways, like the children's perspectives in this story?

Celebrating Juneteenth

I think that Juneteenth is a necessary moment of observation because our government and, to a certain degree, our nation and our culture has not really acknowledged the trauma of 4 million enslaved people and their descendants.
—Author and scholar Karlos Hill

In our daily life with children, families, and all of the school's community, we have to build a way of being together that includes multiple perspectives. It is important in growing the practices and curriculum of our beloved community to stay centered with our values. We carefully consider this when making decisions about what to celebrate or whom to honor in our program.

For example, we have chosen not to celebrate Columbus Day. Instead, we want to honor the First Persons of this nation, who existed long before colonization and are members of the children's community. We celebrate Indigenous Peoples' Day and honor the Muscogee children and families who lived, loved, and thrived on this land before their violent removal. Also, several years ago we began to celebrate Juneteenth Day, offering a divergent perspective on what freedom means. We sent the following message to families to explain our feelings and beliefs surrounding Juneteenth.

A Letter to Families: Why We Celebrate Juneteenth Day

We strive to design and construct a curriculum that reflects the identity of our families and our shared values, including moments of acknowledgment and observance. Times that we collectively find joy in the celebration of life, transitions, the changes of the seasons, and freedom. We thoughtfully consider what celebrations or holidays are meaningful and relevant to children, educators, and families.

Shortly after the Fourth of July in 2017, several educators and I pondered over what Independence Day meant to us personally and as a community. We had little connection to a day exclusively honoring the independence of white landowning men from Britain while our ancestors remained enslaved and/or were experiencing land removal and genocide. That reflection sparked our desire to acknowledge Juneteenth Day and share our perspective with a diverse community.

As a young child, growing up in Milwaukee, Wisconsin, some of Rukia's fondest memories were of the community's Juneteenth Day celebration. For days they celebrated with music, storytelling, poetry, food, and dancing. It was an affirmation of their identity and an acknowledgment of the struggle for freedom. It was part of the Black culture, but was not reflected in the school or textbooks or the dominant culture.

At the Highlander School we have the chance to create a different kind of community, one where we truly value different perspectives and share a broader picture of American history.

Our Juneteenth celebrations and conversations include Black history, folklore, stories, and music. We also pay special attention to the culinary contributions of the diaspora of Africans. For our oldest children, questions around race, slavery, and freedom often arise.

As we approach our Juneteenth celebrations, we think deeply together about conversations to have with the children about why the holiday is a special celebration for Blacks living in the United States. We wrestle with many questions before having these conversations.

- What are the ages of the children?
- What is their understanding and points of views about community, race, and fairness?
- How do we challenge their thinking about misunderstanding?
- What kinds of conversations are taking place at home?

- We know children of color have many conversations with their family about race.
- How do we help white families be more comfortable having these conversations?
- How do we ensure that we don't reinforce stereotypes?
- How do we not cause harm?
- How do we make sure we don't use the children in our group as examples of the stories we are telling?
- How do we offer children empowerment and hope as we share these troubling stories of injustice?

Teachers Estefhaney and Tori shared with our school community how they told the story of Juneteenth to a group of older preschoolers. They explained that a long time ago some people were taken from their homes in Africa, shipped to different parts of the world, and forced to do hard work for others without being paid or treated fairly. For years, Blacks and people who had brown skin were treated unkindly by those in power, who almost always had white skin. During this time people were forced to do whatever they were told even if they did not want to.

Families were separated from one another, and men, women, and even small children were forced to work for long hours doing very hard and sometimes dangerous jobs. Sometimes the enslaved people were hurt very badly or even killed. The educators shared stories of resistance and how abolitionists fought to end slavery. They explained that in June 1865, the last of the enslaved people in rural parts of Texas finally got news that the Civil War was over and Abraham Lincoln's Emancipation Proclamation had declared that all people enslaved in Southern states were to be freed (except under certain provisions of the Thirteenth Amendment and other circumstances). It was a time of celebration for the formerly enslaved. Their memory is honored by celebrating their sacrifices, creativity, resilience, and power!

The children connected their thoughts from conversations about Dr. King and his messages of peace, love, and equity for all people. Estefhaney and Tori explained how this celebration is important because it is crucial to remember times that were challenging and how people can make changes together.

The Juneteenth celebration also brought forth new questions about liberation and freedom, as they can be challenging concepts to explain. What does freedom mean? How do the stories of Juneteenth and emancipation connect with our struggles today that children bear witness to?

Ms. Tracy and her band kicked off the celebration with some songs, but Aria was the friend to get the party started. While the band played "This Little Light of Mine," she jumped up and started dancing to the music. She danced by herself until a few more friends joined in. Lynn also kicked off her own performance, requesting the band play "Jingle Bells." Ms. Tracy handed her the mic, and she said, "Ready, let's go, 1, 2, 1, 2, 1, 3!" She began bobbing to the music while holding the microphone. It was a great celebration as we came together, spreading joy and love through music. The band played songs about love, freedom, peace, and being a family.

Our celebrations at the Highlander School, including Juneteenth, are often times for provocative explorations and questions. Every year as a school we also celebrate Martin Luther King Day. Leading up to his day we talk about who he was, what he stood for, and why people remember him today. Just as Juneteenth delves into the concepts of freedom and enslavement, the Dr. King celebration calls on us to go deeper in helping the children to have the language to describe unfairness as it relates to racial discrimination.

One year we challenged ourselves to dig a little bit further in focusing on our anti-bias goals, not just scratching the surface by talking about Dr. King for a day without further study. Our goal was to have more than surface-level conversations surrounding the importance of activists and activism. Read more stories in chapter 7 about our deeper approaches to Martin Luther King Day.

Listen to another story of celebration from the Highlander School that embodies our values.

Questions for Reflection

What do you already know and understand about Juneteenth?

How might you approach difficult conversations with children about injustice?

What barriers may you have as you begin your work with children?

What do you need to do to begin having conversations about celebrating Juneteenth in your program?

What can you learn from how the Highlander School celebrates Juneteenth?

Our Birthday Celebrations

A new baby is like the beginning of all things—wonder, hope, a dream of possibilities. In a world that is cutting down its trees to build highways, losing its earth to concrete . . . babies are almost the only remaining link with nature, with the natural world of living things from which we spring.

—Author and educator Eda J. LeShan

A child's birth represents infinite possibilities, hopes, dreams, and links between the past and the future. We are born from connections and from this earth. Lost in this fast-paced world of commercialism are the ways in which we once created rituals and traditions to mark the passage of our years on the earth.

- What would it mean to celebrate our births with reverence and interconnection within the entire community?
- What does it mean and what could it feel like to live in community and be known and embraced full well?
- What could a sense of belonging and contribution to others look and feel like?

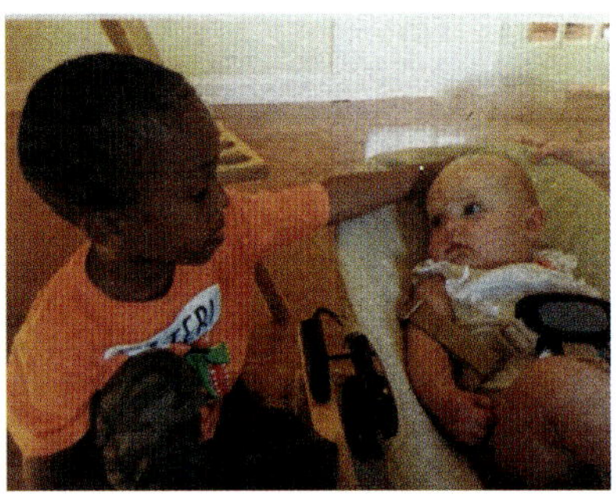

These thoughts and questions guided our approach to building birthday rituals and establishing ongoing traditions to thoughtfully come together to honor our birthdays.

Our birthday traditions have become celebrations of the unique identity of each child as a member of our community, promoting a sense of belonging and meaningful contribution. We value and appreciate each child's existence on this earth within their interconnected relationships. We want to be a place where everyone is known fully, so we honor each child's and staff member's birthday by celebrating with the whole community. Staff celebrations have varied from year to year but include handmade gifts from the children and expressions of love from the families and colleagues.

We wanted to invent new traditions and rituals with the children's voices as an integral piece of our decision-making process. With this in mind, each room creates a provocation with images of the birthday person, inviting everyone from the entire school to create gifts and messages for this special person. Children are invited to work in small groups to generate gifts related to the birthday child's identity as well as to prepare a birthday treat. We listen deeply to what the children know about one another. We believe that working in small groups to prepare gifts also generates solidarity.

The child who is the focus of the celebration feels loved and special. But just as important, the children who take time to create special gifts and messages are filled with pride and love as they think carefully about the birthday person and hope that what they offer will be well received.

Read the following stories as a window into our birthday celebrations.

A Gift for Margot's First Birthday

Today Ms. LaTisha invited preschoolers Elliot and Laylah to the infant living room to help design the cover of a book for Margot's first birthday. Elliot chose the front cover and Laylah wanted to work on the back cover. The children thoughtfully chose which color marker to use. As Elliot considered his choice, he asked, "What's Margot favorite color?" Ms. LaTisha replied, "I'm not sure. I wonder if you could ask Margot about her favorite color."

Elliot decided to use the yellow marker and drew a picture of Margot. Laylah worked quietly with a black marker and made a large circle, adding smaller circles inside. We wondered what she was thinking as she focused on her creation.

Margot came over to investigate what was happening at the table. The children described the drawings as they worked, perhaps to share their perspectives with Margot. "This is a big log. I'm now going to do some moss," Elliot offered as he began to make green circles inside the log. "Those little green dots are moss," he explained. Laylah turned her paper over and exclaimed, "I made a #1," understanding that this was Margot's first birthday. Margot was attentive to their words, nodding her head as though to say she agreed.

The children further described their creations to Ms. LaTisha and Margot.

Elliot: All those little pokie dots are confetti. And those are rocks going up the side of the hill. That's the blue sky and the sun. Umm, Margot is playing outside, the purple is footprints. Another hill. A log with moss, those are decorations.

Laylah: I draw a birthday cake with Margot on it. Rainbow on the back. I did different colors, purple and blue, red. I was trying to do white but it didn't work.

Another time, Vivian and Syrai worked together with Olivia to prepare muffins as part of a celebration. Working in groups strengthens the children's relationships. Our collective efforts and traditions thread together the fashioning of gifts, the preparation of a sensual treat, and our sharing of stories, singing, and dancing.

The Birthday Celebration

The highlight of the birthday tradition is when families join us on the day of the festival and we learn about each family's identity. What is the family story of how it came to be? How and where did the family members come

The Family's Perspective

Being new parents to the Highlander School community, I didn't know what to expect at Olivia's birthday celebration, but I was pleasantly surprised. The whole community of children came together and showered her with songs, gifts, hugs, and attention. This celebration is worth more than any cupcakes and balloons. We are so thankful to be in a school where everyone knows our baby's name.
—Jennifer, Olivia's mom

I really enjoyed the birthday celebration mainly because it brings all of the children together for the birthday child's special day. It does this without causing too much unnecessary hoopla from the parents and outsiders. It emphasizes how unique and special each child is, and we truly appreciate this.
—Nyche, Olivia's dad

together? What does the family like to do together? We incorporate this information into an elaborate story, full of call-and-response songs, about how the birthday child came to be in this world. These culminating birthday celebrations are a joyful thread that brings us together as a community through the arts of song, dance, storytelling, gift giving, and love!

Questions for Reflection

What is your response to the Highlander School's approach to birthday celebrations?

How might the children feel about their birthday celebration?

How might the children who contribute to the celebration feel?

How could your program's practices, rituals, and traditions cultivate a sense of belonging and encourage meaningful contributions in your program?

More Than the Human Community

Children show us in many, many ways their desire to connect to the world and living beings around them. Their attention to the world is expansive, looking beyond human beings to fluidly include the natural world and the universe, with no hierarchy of importance. We know that our ancestors had skills and dispositions that connected them to the natural world in ways that we have lost. They understood and had relationships with the land and the sky, the stars, and the moon. They used these to measure the passage of time, to celebrate, revere, and navigate their world.

These skills are mostly lost to modern adults. But when we look closely, we can see they still reside in the souls of young children. It is a great loss that many of these skills and dispositions are taught out of children. We've told children to look first to the tools of modern technology to make meaning of life. Instead we can look to children to be reminded of more life-affirming ways to be in relationship with our world. As Eda J. LeShan reminds us in *The Conspiracy against Childhood*, "Babies are almost the only remaining link with nature, with the natural world of living things from which we spring"—a link between the past and present.

Listen to the following story to be reminded of how children continually show their innate relationships with and interest in the bigger phenomena of this earth.

"The Mother of the Moon"

Sky our Grandfather
Moon our Grandmother
Earth our Mother
I am thankful
We love each other
We are grateful

—Adapted from a Cherokee prayer

We have noticed that our children often excitedly point when they sight the moon during the day. This morning, we shared with the children that today was the birth of a new moon.

Cora B, age four, had an idea: "We should celebrate and have a baby shower."

Both curious and yearning to support Cora's right to expression, we invited her to share her thinking through the languages of drawing and painting.

Cora B moved with great intentionality, carefully drawing shapes and lines to tell her story. Once finished, she added layers of watercolors to her drawing. Cora shared her picture with Ms. Rukia and described the various elements.

Cora B: "This is the mother of the moon. She has brown skin and braids. There's rain above her head. And here is the baby moon inside her stomach, and this is the grown moon in the sky. And there's one present on each side of her. Ms. Rukia, she looks like you."

When adding the watercolor to the baby moon, she chose to cover it up. Did Cora understand that a new moon cannot be seen?

Cora B showed us that she clearly had a concept of birth and was inspired by our cultural rituals around the birthing celebrations and the welcoming of a new being. Additionally, she reaffirmed the ways in which children see themselves in relationship with all beings and the universe.

Cora B shared her knowledge of the ways to welcome a birth. Let's hear another story related to children joining in the welcome of new members to our community.

Welcoming the Trees

Our Declaration of Intent one year called us to lean into our values and our commitment to creating a more sustainable relationship with this earth. As a community, we were guided by the question, "How do children view the rights of the natural world?" We made plans to enhance our play-scape with fruit trees and native plants. The families and members of the larger community organized to help. As we prepared our minds and souls for this work, we wanted to uphold the perspective of the child and honor the ways in which children contribute to our community.

We imagined the children's response to returning to the school and finding a space different from before. On the workday we told the children about the plants that would be planted and explored the space. Witnessing the children's "empathy for the trees," Ms. LaTisha asked them these questions:

- What do the trees need to feel welcomed here?
- What do the trees need to feel love here?

The children had many ideas:

Hunter: Hugs.

Ellison: Hugs on the tree.

Jace: Medicine.

Cooper: And water.

Ellison: And sun.

Eve: We could give the trees lots of love and we could come out every day to check to see if it's here or not.

Ms. LaTisha: What do the trees need to feel welcome at the Highlander School?

Margot: Water.

Ellison: Love. Good stuff.

Jace: Good stuff.

Ms. LaTisha: Good stuff?

Eve: We could make a sign that says there are trees, there are fruit trees, there are a lot of stuff you could eat.

Margot: They need toys. I can give them my lovie.

Jace: But not too big or you will hurt the tree.

Margot: Yeah, we can make a small toy for the tree.

Hunter: I'll make a robot for the tree. I'll put his arm on the tree. His arm on the arm. I'll make it steady.

Ms. LaTisha: Steady for who?

Hunter: The robot, the tree, and me.

Margot: If we give them hugs and kisses, they will be happy.

We studied the children's responses and the process they took to understand the depth of their connections with the trees, not only to offer what we would consider basic human rights, but to show they believed trees had a right to comforts such as a lovie or toy and that trees expressed emotions. Their answers were ancestral, reflecting their innate understandings, indicating to us they were drawing on our Native ancestors' beliefs.

Drawings for the Trees

Our challenge isn't so much to teach children about the natural world, but to find ways to sustain the instinctive connections they already carry.

—Nature writer Terry Krautwurst

We invite children to draw portraits to nurture connections and other ways of "seeing" all members of our community fully. We believe there is a spiritual connection between children and nature, and our role is to nourish it with love, rich environments, and time.

When the teachers invited the children to draw their ideas about welcoming the trees, they responded with enthusiasm, creating hearts, robots, and toys as offerings to welcome the trees. The next day, without prompting from an adult, several children drew portraits of the trees. Children watched others and the process of drawing unfolded, sparking a collective interest.

Ellison decided to sing to the tree to welcome it. We found her on the playscape, her hands clasped together, singing to the tree.

Questions for Reflection

What is your response to this story about inviting the children to welcome the trees?

What perspectives do you hear in the children's words?

How do you see children's connections to the phenomena of this larger world in your program?

What stories of the sun, stars, moon, rainbows, trees, and wonders of the universe do the children you work with notice?

4 Eagerness for Relationships

It is the image of the child who, from the moment of birth, is so engaged in developing a relationship with the world, and intent on experiencing the world that he or she develops a complex system of abilities, learning strategies and ways of organizing relationships.
—Educator Loris Malaguzzi

At the Highlander School, we carefully observe the children to learn about ways they endeavor to be in relationship with others. We always focus on their interests, personalities, preferences, and aversions while they engage with others. Every day, children show us in a multitude of ways their beautiful and energetic openness for relationships and their strategies for living together in a community. It is our hope that the stories offered here will spark your own view of children's competence and encourage your efforts to support their natural abilities as you notice how children are eager and able to make connections with others.

The Tree Is Dying

While on the playscape, Ellison approached Rukia with a look of worry on her face.

Ellison: Ms. Rukia, I have to show you something!

Ellison waved her arm and beckoned Rukia to follow her.

Ellison: I need to show you the tree.

Rukia followed her until she stopped in front of the tree and pointed toward its branches. Rukia knew that the tree had been ill for some time.

Ellison: It's dying! Look . . . there's no leaves on the branches. Look at the top of the tree. There's no leaves!

Ms. Rukia: Yes I see. What should we do about it?

Ellison: Water. I think it needs water.

Using the water hose, Ellison gently offered water to the tree. She soon shared the story of the tree with the other children, and collective concern grew. Several of the children began to lay hands on the tree, rubbing and hugging the tree. "I'm rubbing the tree cause I want to take care of it," Francis whispered.

Rukia wondered who had taught the children to hug the tree. She considered the ways that children innately seek to be in relationship with others, recognizing the power of touch to connect, embrace, and console others. The children of the Highlander School are held and hugged every day, and they were using the same strategies to help the tree.

This story demonstrates how we need to reframe our image of young children and the role we play with them in these moments. Young children are far from being self-centered, and their actions are much more than merely "cute." Rather, they are deeply connected to and compassionate about the world around them. Does our way of teaching teach this out of them? Our work on healing the environment and our humanity begins with children's compassion and desire for relationships with all living things. You can't save what you don't love.

Human beings have a vital stake in developing relationships. From birth, children depend on relationships within their world to survive and thrive. It makes sense that, as Loris Malaguzzi suggests above, they have an innate drive to develop complex systems and abilities, learning strategies, and ways of seeking, understanding, and building relationships.

Good Morning

A baby is born to use their clever and imitative human nature to develop as a "person in relationship," seeking knowledge and skills that have meaning for other people. That is how we learn.

—Attributed to child psychologist Colwyn Trevarthen

As children arrive each morning, the dance of fostering relationships unfolds. Eager, curious faces light up when friends see one another. There are exchanges of warm greetings and welcoming touches. Some children are more tentative about saying goodbye to their families, so the adults step in with outstretched hands and comforting embraces. Even the youngest children move in to care for their friends in this tender moment.

When we pause to notice these seemingly ordinary exchanges, we see the best of humanity come to light. In these moments we know we are meant to feel a sense of belonging and we understand that we seek reciprocal relationships with others and with life.

Really seeing each other is more than just saying "hey" and moving on to the day. It's a vital experience of recognition and acknowledgment. It is important that all beings are fully seen, heard, and known, so we honor each member's integral role in our world. This is especially true for children and families whose cultural identity does not reflect that of the dominant white and Western culture. This is true for Black and Brown children,

Questions for Reflection

What is your response to the idea that children are born as a "person in relationship," seeking knowledge and skills that have meaning for other people?

What have you seen children do that shows their eagerness to connect with others?

children of recent immigrants, and families experiencing housing insecurity, whose perspectives may not be understood nor cherished by the larger community and systems of oppression. We acknowledge children's eagerness to be in relationship with others, and our role as the beloved community is to ensure that these relationships flourish from a place of authenticity and deep connections.

An absence of positive identity development and appreciation for diversity, along with economic insecurities caused by institutional racism and oppression, has a profound negative effect on children and the world we live in. Black and Brown children are marginalized in white Western culture, and representation of people of color is often missing or given a negative light. This affects all children's views of themselves and others. Children are continually studying others to learn more about them. They notice similarities and differences from the time they are babies. All children come to us with curiosity about others, eagerness to connect, and innate competencies for seeking and developing relationships. They deserve to feel a sense of belonging and to join in welcoming others. We can make a difference if we question our own assumptions and reflect on our practices with children to ensure we notice, celebrate, and support children's individual identities, dispositions, and competencies for connection and caring.

The many ways people welcome and greet one another across cultural groups can inspire us. The South African greeting "Sawubona" means "I see you" in Zulu. The response is, "Yebo, Sawubona," "I see you too." This generous recognition of each other is significant in building a sense of belonging and interdependence. Children are born with this desire to see others and be seen. Understanding and making visible the simple yet profound ways children remind us of this desire can nourish and transform our work, our lives, and our world.

When we observe children's actions and engagement closely, we notice them seeking to answer questions about their identity, about others, about where they belong, about how they will be cared for, and about how they can contribute. They may be seeking answers to questions like:

- Who am I in relationship to the people and the world around me?
- How will I learn about others? How will I learn about my world?
- How can I contribute to others?
- How can I respond to others in ways that build our connections?
- How do I belong to this family and community?

- Who are these people, and how are we alike and different?
- What does my family, community, and larger world tell me about myself and other people? Who is worthy and important?

Children's intense study of us and their world offers both vital responsibilities and meaningful possibilities for adults who strive to create a more compassionate, equitable world through our work with young children. The good news is that children have natural dispositions and skills to bring to this work, and adults can recognize these and call on them to strengthen children's compassionate identities as we endeavor to build a better world.

"These Are All My Friends!"

The friends of our friends are our friends.

—Attributed to a Congolese proverb

The three-year-old children immediately stopped what they were doing to notice Deb, a new visitor to the playground. Curious to find out more and connect with this new person, several children smiled and said hello. Deb answered with a cheery greeting. Determining that she was friendly, a few children approached her to engage, while the others attentively observed the unfolding interactions.

Cooper showed her a scar on his palm. Sunny gently held up a worm that was wriggling in her hand. Obinna sang out "Hello" and with a sweeping gesture toward the group, announced, "These are all my friends!" Using his finger to point to each child, he began counting from one to ten. Deb responded, "You have so many friends." "Yes," he joyfully replied, and showed her several tricks, rolling, jumping, and spinning his body around.

When you observe children while watching for the skills and dispositions they already have for cultivating relationships, it is clear how socially aware and tuned in they are to the people and events happening around

Questions for Reflection

How does this story reflect the idea that children are eager for relationships?

In what ways do the children try to get to know Deb and have her know them?

What experiences have you had where children showed interest in getting to know you? What did they do? How did you respond?

them. Yet the dominant narrative focuses on children as individuals, rather than as important members of the community. Often the stories adults tell about children suggest a lack of social abilities. Children are often described as self-centered, egocentric, needy, and unable to share or take turns. These ideas about children's lack of social competencies are widespread and are at odds with the capable young humans we heard about in the above story, who are striving to belong and connect. When adults view children only as individuals, incompetent in their social encounters, we jump in to teach them or scold them, which undermines their natural gifts.

The children's ordinary actions in the story reflect a genuine desire to belong as members of a community. We can see this in their immediate attentiveness to Deb's presence in the yard and in the way they greeted her and studied her to decide whether she was a friendly person.

Once they determined Deb was amiable and interested in them, they easily found ways to share themselves. Cooper trusted that Deb would care about the injury on his hand. Sunny invited her to appreciate the remarkable creature she was holding, and Obinna encouraged her to join in a celebration of his many friends and offered a gift of skillful body movements. At such a young age, the children already understand what brings people together—empathy, shared curiosity, exuberance, and the joys of friendship. The children truly believe the phrase, "your friends are my friends."

Questions for Reflection

What is your view of children's social competencies?

Do you see them first as individuals or as members of the community?

How might the way you see children in these moments influence your responses to them? How might your responses influence their development as caring, interdependent human beings?

Children Are Present

William Schafer offers his view of children's remarkable abilities in "The Infant as Reflection of the Soul." He suggests that children are born with three spiritual dimensions that most of us no longer experience as adults, which many people try to reclaim through spiritual practices such as prayer and meditation. He describes these as:

Presence: approaching others with pure pleasure and awareness, free from judgment, comparison, or fear.

Joy: a strong sense of being drawn toward someone in wonder, curiosity, and interest.

Awareness of others' awareness: the realization that we are not alone, exhilarated with the idea that we share awareness with others, and that others exist who are present to our experiences.

Do you hear the wisdom of the South African greeting "I see you," "I see you too" reflected in Schafer's view of children? Bringing this view to your observations of children can enhance your appreciation for the everyday moments you often take for granted and help you realize that they are deeply meaningful. Respecting children in this way will also transform how you respond, calling on children's natural desire to belong rather than believing you have to jump in and teach them.

Study the following stories to look for more details showing children's natural dispositions for presence, joy, and awareness.

Welcoming Zola

The windows that open up the physical spaces of the Highlander School invite community members to see one another and feel connected all the time, so the news of a new community member travels fast. The children are particularly interested in the babies, checking through the windows to see what's up each time they pass. Today many children from the different age groups were looking forward to meeting new baby Zola. Two babies in her own group made advances throughout the day, moving in to look closely at her face and interacting with smiles and friendly vocal greetings. Seeing she was a younger baby, both were eager to care for Zola. Ellie showed curiosity in Zola's pacifier, as she uses one too, and Callan wanted to help feed her a bottle. Zola responded to their attention, moving her legs and arms excitedly, showing interest and pleasure. Zola definitely felt welcomed by these new friends.

Later that morning, when the children were outside, others came to greet Zola. Millie from the preschool room yelled to her friend, referring to the baby, "Isn't she adorable?" They joined together with Zola on a blanket and began to talk, touch, and play with her. Several other children came over to meet and bond with this new friend. Zola turned toward them smiling, showing delight in response to the attention.

Bouncing Baby Beau

Zola took time to interact with the new baby Beau today, maybe remembering and reciprocating the warm welcome she received several months earlier. Beau was sitting in the bouncy chair and Zola came over, placed her hands on the chair, and began to gently move it up and down. The movement of the chair captured Beau's attention, and he looked at Zola, giving her a big smile. As Zola continued to move the bouncer, she discovered Beau's socks and started to pull at them. This action excited Beau and the two gave each other more big smiles. Zola has been practicing standing by herself, and this interaction with Beau motivated her to keep standing and enjoy the moment while holding on to his socks. Beau didn't seem to mind. Ellie came over to join the fun. She began to bounce Beau's chair too, and the children all shared big smiles as their relationships grew.

Looking through the Blocks

The toddlers spent time this morning stacking and balancing colorful translucent blocks to build a tower of windows. Getting the blocks to balance was a tricky task, but they stuck with it and had many successes. However, what we noticed most about this experience was the way the children were drawn to peek through the block windows. Several children came over and they took turns moving around the table, joyously smiling and laughing at the simple, yet deeply nourishing notion that they could see one another through the blocks!

Questions for Reflection

Revisit the stories above. Study the photos of the children engaged with one another. How are they showing their eagerness to be in relationship?

How are they showing they care about each other and want to help?

What do you notice about their skills using facial expressions and body language? What do you imagine their vocalizations and tone of voice are communicating?

What do you guess they are noticing and learning as they interact and imitate each other?

The Compassionate Instinct

Bringing people together is what I call "ubuntu," which means "I am because we are." Far too often people think of themselves as just individuals, separated from one another, whereas you are connected and what you do affects the whole world. When you do well it spreads out, it is for the whole of humanity.

—Widely attributed to Bishop Desmond Tutu

The children in the stories above understand that "we are all connected and what we do affects the whole world," as Desmond Tutu suggests.

At the Highlander School we regularly observe how children use many ways to invite interdependence. It is common for children to share of themselves while offering invitations for their community members to join together. Children seek these connections by noticing one another and acting with generosity, concern, and care.

Science tells us that young humans are born with a compassionate instinct. This instinct is a product of our evolution, as we need to look out for one another for our species to survive. It is no wonder children come ready to grow these instincts.

Children feel sympathy when they *understand* what another person is feeling. Children's own emotional experiences offer them the opportunity to see and understand these feelings in another. Empathy is when a child actually *feels* what another is feeling. Compassion comes from feeling sympathy and empathy. When you are compassionate, you feel the pain of another (empathy) or you recognize that the person is in pain (sympathy), and then you want to help that person. Compassion releases hormones in our brains that give us good feelings, so we naturally behave in these ways. Compassion is the drive to want to help and our motivation for activism.

In a society that is often fast paced, competitive, rigorous, and individualistic, have adults lost this compassionate instinct and are they unable to see it in others? Perhaps adults don't notice compassionate behaviors in young children because their actions are often very subtle. Dominant theories about young children perpetuate the notion that children are selfish and self-centered so we need to teach them to care and share, so this is the story we tell about what we see.

Sympathy, empathy, and compassion are generated from our souls and connections. It is the role of the adults and educators to nourish these expressions and create optimal learning environments. It is not our desire for children to look outside of themselves for how to behave—rather, we hope they can call on their own innate understandings.

Because the children's offerings of compassion are subtle, we must look closely for them and make their competencies visible to help us understand their perspective and human development. Imagine a world where we notice, support, and are inspired by these young humans' strong compassionate instinct. The world as we know it could look very different.

Study the following stories to practice seeing these subtle, yet profound moments between children.

Tender Attention

Love is an action.

—Author and educator bell hooks

The children in our infant room were curious about Cecilia, the new child who was now the youngest in the community. Zora was particularly interested and carefully observed Cecilia. She crawled over to the mat where Cecilia was lying and began to look at her. She continued to look at her as if trying to really know Cecilia and take in her every essence. Cecilia accepted this invitation and gazed back with curious attention. Zora moved in closer to Cecilia, gently tracing her head with her fingers. Their eyes connected and Cecilia smiled. Zora leaned in for a sweet embrace and a kiss on the check. Cecilia smiled, delighted by the gentle touches.

The infant brain is primed to gaze at and respond to kind, caring facial expressions. Most humans have positive responses to gentle, affectionate touches. We see in this story the children's apt attention as they closely look at and respond to offerings from one another. Their curiosity and attention seems to be the beginning of a trusting, affectionate relationship, helping them grow their understandings of compassion. These moments are small, yet significant, so we make sure we notice them and marvel at the children's natural gifts for engaging with tender attention.

Questions for Reflection

What details do you notice in the photos that reflect how the children may be learning about sympathy, empathy, and compassion during this interaction?

When have you noticed children showing one another this kind of tender attention?

Sullivan the Sweet

We witnessed a beautiful moment in which Sullivan showed acts of love and kindness, comforting Penelope during a moment of need. Since her first week with us, we have noticed Sullivan's awareness of the other children and her desire to make physical and emotional connections with her peers. Penelope has been struggling with being away from her family, and Sullivan has been paying close attention to Penelope's sadness. Sullivan responded with compassion and offered a gentle hug. Through a touch of her hand or a kind gesture, Sullivan has become one of our room comforters.

Nonverbal Communication

Each of us walks around in the world making meaning of what we see, hear, and experience. We have an amazing capacity to take in information and instantly make sense of it. From infancy we have learned to interpret the people and events happening around us. We discover that facial expressions and body language give us reams of information. The tone of someone's voice creates more understanding. As adults, we instantly size up a situation without even realizing what factors are influencing us. And each of us does this in a different way, with the different filters of our family culture, childhood, temperament, and experiences.

As you read the details of the children's competencies for relationships in the stories above, did you notice how effectively they communicated with limited verbal language? Children have remarkable skills in understanding nonverbal communication, including body language, facial expressions, and tone of voice, which they use to learn about others and grow relationships. Unlike adults, they are still engaged in carefully studying and making meaning of what they see and experience. They pay close attention to both understanding and using this kind of communication.

While adults use nonverbal communication unconsciously, children, as researcher Alison Gopnik suggests in *The Philosophical Baby* and her other work, are scientists closely paying attention to people to learn how this back-and-forth dance of making meaning works. Gopnik's research suggests that very young children actually perform complex statistical analyses and make predictions about how people will respond through their skillful study of communication exchanges. As children make these predictions correctly, adults often characterize them as "being manipulative" rather than seeing the remarkable abilities children are using for communicating.

Observing for children's nonverbal communication will help you become more responsive and strengthen your image of their competencies. And because the way you communicate with children has such a huge impact on their growing identity and understanding of relationships, studying children's and your own nonverbal habits is critical to your work.

Be mindful of cultural considerations when it comes to nonverbal communication. Eye contact varies across cultures, as does the amount of personal space people feel comfortable maintaining. Being aware of how families and children communicate with one another will offer you more information and appreciation for differences between cultures and the role you can play to support diverse styles.

Consider these questions for reflection about nonverbal communication as you study the story and photos of the children and teacher that follow:

- How are the children and teacher using their bodies, gestures, and touches to communicate?
- How do the children and teacher communicate using facial expressions and eye contact?
- What do you imagine their vocalizations and tone of voice are communicating?
- How might this nonverbal communication be growing compassion?

Who Enjoys Avocado Toast?

It's breakfast time and Ms. Jamesha sits down with the children to share in the pleasure of food. She carefully notices each of the children's facial expressions as they take their first bites of the avocado toast. Beck's facial expression shows displeasure. Ms. Jamesha's expression is accepting as she uses a gentle tone of voice to acknowledge her understanding, "You don't like the avocado toast, Beck." She shows empathy while trying to encourage him to try again by taking her own bite and showing her enjoyment through a pleased expression. He continues to communicate his dissatisfaction through his face, also offering a clear gesture of resistance by using his fingers to cover his month and maybe even comfort himself. Ms. Jamesha really listens to Beck's communication, accepts his message, and cheerfully offers him a piece of plain toast with butter. He willingly accepts the new toast.

Mira has a different response. She shows Ms. Jamesha that she is enjoying the toast with her smiling face and by lifting the toast toward Ms. Jamesha to show her delight in their shared appreciation for the yummy toast. Ms. Jamesha next makes sure she includes Mike in this nonverbal dance by turning to him and offering him a warm smile and pointing to the toast they are enjoying together.

Ms. Jamesha shows respectful attention to the children's nonverbal cues. Her own nonverbal communication is warmhearted and beautiful. You can see the gentleness and grace in her hands and gestures and feel the empathy, compassion, and warmth radiating from her facial expressions.

Love and Care Are Essential

We yearn to end the lovelessness that is so pervasive in our society.

—Author and educator bell hooks

Jamesha's attention to her communication with the babies is fundamental in growing their compassionate instinct. Caring adults who take children's ideas and feelings seriously provide the most essential support for children's development while nourishing their own lives. There is a long history of the ethics of love and care in the early childhood profession. bell hooks has provided a powerful and visionary voice for the work we are doing at the Highlander School to grow the beloved community. Diminishing and undervaluing care and love in all aspects of our lives, from the youngest members of our community to the oldest, can never create a flourishing, more just world.

Care and compassion are expressed in small ways throughout our days with children. Enjoy the following brief stories and photos that reflect these small moments that are imbued with so much significance for children's well-being and the development of their empathy and compassion.

These small stories highlight how the Highlander School community members show care and concern as well as their joy in being together.

The Comfort of a Lap

Hunter was upset. He shared with Ms. Jessica that he missed his family. Ms. Jessica is sensitive and responsive to his feelings. She held Hunter close to her. He leaned in, relaxing his body and placing his elbow on her lap. Ms. Jessica brought out a picture that showed Hunter and his family visiting the aquarium. She invited Hunter to share stories of what was unfolding in the picture. Hunter is avid in studying animals and has become an expert about so many. Ms. Jessica's welcoming lap, tender touch, and reassuring tone of voice offered soothing comfort for Hunter in the moment.

I Know, I Understand

Wystan, known lovingly by our community as Wyt Wyt, emerged from the bathroom with tears streaming down his face. He was overwhelmed with grief and called for his mother.

Ms. LaTisha leaned in, placing her hand on his chest.

Ms. LaTisha: What's wrong, Wyt Wyt?

Wystan: I want my mama.

Ms. LaTisha: I know; I understand.

Ms. LaTisha sat with Wystan on the couch for a long time. Hearing his cries, the other children joined in consoling him. It was Wystan's second day since returning to the Highlander School after eight months away. Like so many other young children, Wystan had been home for a prolonged period of time because of the COVID-19 pandemic, isolated from people outside his household.

Ms. LaTisha was keenly aware of Wystan's despair and yearning to be with his family, as well as his desire to feel secure. It is the right of the child, and any human, to be able to sit with their feelings and process emotions of discomfort. Ms. LaTisha made no attempt to silence Wystan's cries. He held strong bonds and attachments with his mother and family, and it was logical and healthy that he wanted to be with them. Our role in creating a beloved community is to validate those feelings; empathize with children; and offer sincere, loving compassion.

You're Hurt

Hunter injured his hand while playing on our playscape one morning. Ms. Rukia responded quickly to his big tears and loud cries of pain. Lovingly she offered, "Let's go and take care of that so you will feel better." Ms. LaTisha joined them with the first aid supplies. Both adults leaned in close to Hunter, consoling him by enclosing him between them and using gentle words. Ms. LaTisha suggested that Hunter could look at his cut and describe what she was doing to help him. Hunter's crying subsided as he leaned in to the comfort of their closeness to study what she was doing.

Typical childhood injuries offer perfect opportunities for children to feel compassionate care. Children come to trust they will be taken care of and see that with help from others we all can get through hard times. And when adults care for children, it reinforces children's natural desire to care for others.

A Gentle Kiss

When Cristiano joined our community, he was full of passion, love, and vibrant energy. At home he enjoyed wrestling with his father and attempted to wrestle as a means of entering play with the other children. This approach was not well received by his peers. They often responded

with cries and were visibly displeased. This collective reaction left Cristiano upset and confused, and he often cried as a result. In addition, the other children had already established relationships, since they had been together since they were infants and had multiple ways of knowing one another, which made it even more difficult for Cristiano to join in.

The educators wanted to create a sense of belonging for Cristiano and support his relationships. They planned for him to have an encounter with Jace, a child Cristiano had shown interest in playing with. The educators invited the children to look into a mirror and see themselves together. Upon seeing their side-by-side reflections, they both smiled and laughed. They studied themselves and looked at each other. Cristiano turned to Jace and held Jace's face softly between his hands. He then leaned in and kissed Jace on his forehead. We had noticed that this was the way Cristiano's father held Cristiano's face and kissed him when dropping him off at school. Jace received the warm kiss and returned it with a hug. This ordinary yet rich moment seemed to be the spark for a budding friendship full of love, passion, energy, and the power of touch.

Questions for Reflection

How much do you know about your own nonverbal communication with children? Take some time to study your own style. Consider having someone videotape you so you can study yourself.

What more do you want to understand about children's way of using nonverbal communication?

What new understandings do you have about how your own compassionate, nonverbal communication is central to young children's development of sympathy, empathy, and compassion?

Eagerness for Relationships with Other Living Beings

Children notice and bear witness to all! It is the magic of childhood to see a bird for the first time and acknowledge the simple presence of a tree on this earth. Children are not only drawn to relationships with other humans but also have keen observation skills and deep sensitivity for other living things. Yet children's perspectives and relationships to other beings are often characterized as "cute." The term *anthropomorphism* (the attribution of human traits, emotions, or intentions to nonhuman entities) is often used to describe children's ideas about relationships with other living creatures—basically saying that children only appreciate other living creatures when they pretend they have human characteristics. Yet the more we learn from science about the nature of the nonhuman world, the more we see that children's views have much to offer us. Scientific studies of the nature of trees now showing that they have strong abilities to communicate with other trees and studies examining the ways dogs and cats are connected with humans are good examples. Children and science show us that caring relationships with beings outside our species are possible and even vital for our survival. I believe children see more than we give them credit for and we have much to learn from them, as illustrated in the following stories.

An Encounter with an Ant

The toddlers are often captivated by the insects that live in our playscape. Today there was a collective outcry of excitement as Penelope observed an ant traveling on the bike path and cried out, "Oh no!"

Ava soon joined the excitement observing the ant as it traveled through the grass. As the ant crawled out of sight, Penelope was worried about the ant and repeated, "Oh no!"

The children repositioned their bodies, lying flat on the ground to take a closer look. They tenderly watched the ant for a long time, passionately engaged together in this shared interest and concern. How often do adults walk past an ant without a thought or consideration?

"It's a Lady Bug"

The presence of a ladybug required a collective pause and joyful observations for this group of two-year-olds. As the children carefully moved in closer, making room for everyone to marvel together around this wonderous creature, several children called out.

"It's a ladybug . . . it's getting on my finger!"

"It's going up there!!"

When was the last time you were thrilled about the sight of a ladybug and wanted to share your excitement with the people around you? Children's awe and yearning to connect with the natural world and share with others delights us every day. The children notice the intricate details of nature and engage with respect and reverence. Just as remarkably, they understand that other children share their wonder and appreciation. Joining in the excitement heightens the experience for everyone—and maybe even for the ladybug, if we believe, as the children do, that all living beings are connected in our world!

Questions for Reflection

What is your response to stories of children seeking relationships with the natural world?

What of children's perspectives and understandings of the natural world delights or inspires you?

How do the children's perspectives, eagerness, and care for other living beings affect your views?

What examples do you have of children engaging in studying and caring for the natural world and other living beings in your own life?

What role have you taken up or would you like to take up to support children's instinctive desires and interests in the natural world?

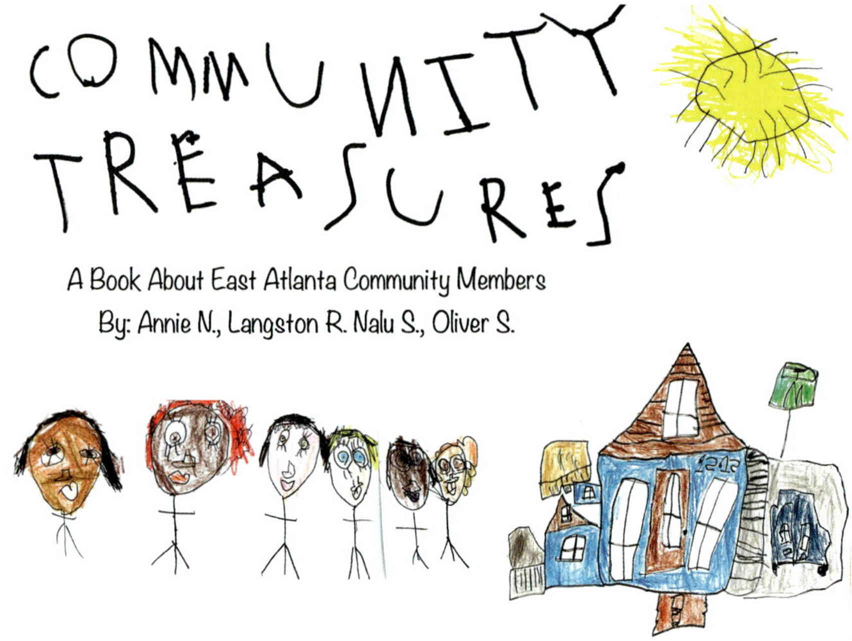

Community Treasures

The new school year had begun with the merger of a toddler room with the multiage room, creating a new dynamic while strengthening existing relationships. The educators were interested in how friendships would form and how the new community and culture would unfold. Ms. Estefhaney and Ms. Bianca share the expansive thinking that children have about being in community together.

With research questions guiding them, the educators pursued an understanding of how the children defined community. Working in small groups, the children were invited to draw their community. Then the educators listened. They noticed that many drawings included the children's immediate family or people who lived in their home. Others held a more expansive definition of community, and their drawings included neighbors, friends, and pets. Some included fictional characters.

Our thinking deepened and a new question emerged. We wondered: How do we help the children expand their sense of community? How would the children navigate expanding their community?

We proposed taking regular walks around the neighborhood to get a closer look at our community. The walks ignited new discussions around the children's observations and what they might want to add to their community drawings.

As the children shared their drawings, their diverse perspectives on what community meant to them were revealed. Langston's viewpoint was that a person could be a part of more than one community. He considered himself to be a part of his neighborhood community and the Highlander School community. Annie expanded her community from herself and family to others at the school. Oliver strongly insisted that the people of Atlanta and everyone else were a part of his community. As we continued our walks, we began talking to people we met, asking them how they saw themselves in the community.

After many walks and discussions, the children decided to add various members of our community to their drawings, including Ms. Trellis, our librarian; Mr. Hunter, our firefighter; Mr. Mookah, a local barista; Ms. Shassidy, a local baker; and Stoney Age, the large tree in a neighbor's yard. The children, with the support of the educators, asked each being for an interview and for permission to make their portrait. The small-group meetings with these community folks gave us the opportunity to pay close attention to the children's ideas about community. The following reflect some of the questions and conversations compiled by Ms. Bianca and Ms. Estefhaney.

Ms. Trellis, the Librarian

Annie: Why do you have to be quiet?

Ms. Trellis: Because it's the library there's no talking in the library because people be studying, some people be on the computer focusing on what they are doing so to stay focused they have to be quiet.

Nalu: What do you like about being a librarian?

Annie: We are going to go around to places, going to ask people in our community questions. And if they say no we will move on to another place.

Ms. Trellis: That's a great idea, and how you will get to know your community, going door to door and you tell them your name and ask them their name and let them know who you are so you can know who they are too. And then you might be able to get to know everyone in your community.

Mr. Mookah, the Barista

Annie: Did you always want to work at the coffee shop?

Mr. Mookah: I don't know; I was always wanting to work with people; I like people.

Nalu: Even strangers?

Mr. Mookah: Even strangers. Strangers if you don't know them you say hello. No one is a stranger; you say hello and get to know them. But I knew I was going to be serving people. But I didn't know I would be in coffee;

coffee was an accident. I started off in banking. And I wanted to do something different so I went back to something I was good at.

Nalu: I can do questions first. Why did you want this to be a coffee shop?

Mr. Mookah: Well people normally start a business because of a demand for something, and a coffee shop was needed in this neighborhood because people wanted coffee. Is that a good answer? (He laughs.) It's all about supply and demand—all businesses go for what the customer wants.

Annie: Do you like your job?

Mr. Mookah: I love my job.

Annie: Because you're working with people.

Mr. Mookah: Part of it is I grew up in this village so I love the people in this village.

Nalu: In Atlanta, Georgia, Flat Shoals.

Mr. Mookah: Yup. Flat Shoals Ave., so it's an honor for me to work in this neighborhood where I grew up.

Ms. Shassidy, the Baker

Annie: Hello, my name is Annie. How do you make chocolate glaze donuts? I really want to make some by myself.

Ms. Shassidy: I really don't know right now. I haven't learned that yet; you'll have to come back in a couple of weeks and ask me and I'll tell you.

Annie: Why do you have bunches of donuts?

Ms. Shassidy: Because people love donuts, and we want to give them a variety. Do you know what my favorite is?

Nalu: Did you build this shop?

Ms. Shassidy: Did I build this shop? No, I didn't build this shop, but this shop has been here for like twenty-six, twenty-seven years.

Nalu: What? That's a long time.

Langston: That's a loonnng time.

This experience was a profound exchange between the children and members of our community, creating the opportunity for each group to be seen and heard. Imagine a world where we are known full well and each of us has a sense of belonging. Oliver's comment on the experience perfectly sums up the beloved community we are striving to create: "Community is like a part of our school, and like cousins, how we love them."

5 Playing, Learning, and Working Together

Play, while it cannot change the external realities of children's lives, can be a vehicle for children to explore and enjoy their differences and similarities and to create, even for a brief time, a more just world where everyone is an equal and valued participant.

—Professor and writer Patricia G. Ramsey

Playing, working, and learning *together* is the natural way humans construct knowledge, share ideas, and live in community. Children's play and work empowers them to make connections with the greater world and make meaning of it. For example, after a recent rally to protect a local forest that the Highlander School children attended, the children re-created the forest in the block area, chanted "don't cut down the trees," and invented powers to protect the trees.

Adults may dismiss these collective endeavors as ordinary events and not give them the attention they deserve. At the Highlander School we actively look for the multiple brilliant ways in which children show us their ability to observe, develop hypotheses, create connections, learn together, and negotiate ideas. We believe children's innate dispositions and skills are a powerful foundation for growing a more nourishing, democratic world.

The Dance of the Dinosaurs

Preschoolers Ellison and Hunter shared space around the table, using several containers filled with warm, sudsy water and several plastic dinosaurs. They spent a short time on their own exploring the sensory elements of the water, dipping the dinosaurs in and out and splashing and moving the water as it spilled over the sides of the bins. Recognizing each other's

actions, they joined to play together in many ways, pushing the dinosaurs under the water until they were fully submerged and transformed with dripping, glistening skin. They also worked together to transport the dinosaurs and the water back and forth between the bins, filling and dumping the containers. Their experience involved exuberant physical movement as they traveled around the table from bin to bin. They naturally joined in pretend play, engaging in intense negotiations using the dinosaurs as characters who talked fiercely to each other about sharing the space and the water. Here is some of what the dinosaurs said:

Dinosaur 1 (Ellison): You can swim in your own water. I need deeper water.

Dinosaur 2 (Hunter): Hey you can't take our water.

Dinosaur 1 (Ellison): Pink water is me.

Dinosaur 2 (Hunter): Can you give me a ride?

Dinosaur 1 (Ellison): Pink is my favorite.

Dinosaur 2 (Hunter): We can both take more water.

Dinosaur 1 (Ellison): Now look who has the most.

Dinosaur 2 (Hunter): Don't do that—you're going to hurt the dinosaur.

Dinosaur 1 (Ellison): I want water. I'm going to take it.

Dinosaur 2 (Hunter): Why you not sharing?

The children's voices were loud, and the interactions between the dinosaurs and their physical movements with each other were rough. The intensity of this play between Hunter and Ellison might lead us to believe that this was a conflict that needed to be resolved or even stopped. The question posed by Hunter was profound and indicative of the ways in which children's play is the embodiment of our joys and struggles in an adult world. How do we share water? How do we share resources?

Neither of the children seemed upset, and they were willing to keep playing this game, despite any tension. Children don't often shy away from conflict and tend to readily forgive transgressions. In contrast, many adults try to avoid conflict and often resolve things passive-aggressively, carrying a grudge or going behind others' backs to complain.

Holding onto our belief in children's innate social competencies, we can pause to consider how this play, as Patricia Ramsey suggests in the quote above, could be a "vehicle for children to explore and enjoy their differences and similarities."

Questions for Reflection

What are your reactions to this dinosaur play?

How might your comfort levels and attitudes toward conflict influence your work with children and other adults?

Culture and Approaches to Play

Ellison and Hunter share similar approaches to this dinosaur play but different dispositions toward working together as the play develops. We can see from Hunter's words to Ellison that he more often invites her to join in the play with him and promotes the idea of sharing, like when he says, "Can you give me a ride?"; "We can both take more water"; and "Why you not sharing?" On the other hand, Ellison shows her independence by standing up for herself and her desire to follow her own ideas.

Their ways of playing are both intuitively and specifically passed down from their family, their culture, and the people they have played with. White-dominant, American culture often promotes individualism and independence, whereas many Indigenous communities foster cooperation and interdependence. The research on children's learning styles identifies these differences as *field dependent* and *field independent* approaches, respectively. Field-dependent children are more group oriented and approach play and learning in a social way. Field-independent children are less reliant on others and more self-motivated.

In this play, the fact that the children approach it differently and stay with it regardless of their differences helps them explore others' perspectives and new ideas for working together. Hunter may try out ways to stand up for his ideas, and Ellison may come to appreciate the value of collaboration.

If we pause to consider the alarming state of diminishing world resources and think about how humans use and share these resources, Hunter's question "Why you not sharing?" is significant. How will we work to resolve the inequity in our own communities around shared resources? How do we examine our own practices and the use of vital resources like water that we need to protect and share? We can follow the children's lead by staying engaged so we can negotiate our differences with equity in mind. We can take up the tension between using materials like water that we value for children's play and the ethical dilemma this poses with the use of a scarce resource. How can we support the children to undertake this work to protect and share resources they naturally care about?

Joining Together to Play

Close observation of children's play through a social competencies lens reveals how their natural play strategies constantly invite opportunities to enhance their relationships. Children instinctively engage in play using similar ideas and actions, and they understand the importance of these similarities for their connections with each other. These mutual approaches afford them opportunities to practice their inherent skills and dispositions for getting along. Consider the following elements and the way they helped children connect with each other during the water and dinosaur play.

Shared Sensory Experiences

Children experience the world through sensual and sensorial means that are both spiritual and informative. This process is the foundation for our connections with the universe and, thus, our brain development and learning. Children have a strong drive to seek these experiences over and over again. Observing children closely, you will see the powerful role this mutual drive plays in their connections with one another. We can study details of this at work in "The Dance of the Dinosaurs" story.

In the dinosaur play, the children shared the pleasure of exploring the gift of water and all her sensory and spiritual elements. Water in this moment appeared to enhance their connection with each other as she has done in the rituals of many cultures throughout time. We can marvel at how both children enjoyed the warm water and billowing suds. They both saw the magic and power of making the water move and change. They centered their shared enjoyment and sought from each other new ideas for engaging with the water. There was deep satisfaction as they realized they could join together in the pleasure of this moment.

Although the children's drama focused on the dinosaurs sharing the water, we called the story "The Dance of the Dinosaurs" because of the way the children moved their bodies in unison as a part of the play. They glided back and forth from one end of the table to the other, noticing each other's bodies as they passed. They never bumped into each other and instead seemed to find a resonance, moving together as if dancing. Although they used aggressive interactions when the dinosaurs rammed into each other, all of the movements seemed choreographed to make sure they didn't hurt each other.

Repeated Actions

Both Ellison and Hunter were eagerly engaged in filling and dumping the containers with the soapy water. They carefully transported the full containers back and forth from bin to bin. They showed rapt attention for immersing the dinosaurs completely under the water, noticing how they transformed the water and the dinosaurs through their actions.

Studies of schema, these repeated actions in children's play, have found them to be innate in children. Children's use of these repeated

Questions for Reflection

How often do you notice how children move together in their play and see their movement as a central part of their social connection?

What do you notice about how children share space, observe each other, and are inspired to move like each other?

explorations is a powerful force for their individual learning and development. Research suggests that these repeated patterns reflect children's brains building connections for understanding the world around them. But maybe even more noteworthy is how these repeated actions support children in playing together even without words or making explicit agreements.

Dramatic Play

Children's pretend play has long been viewed among early childhood researchers and teachers as an avenue for developing social skills. The underlying themes of this kind of play provide opportunities for children to enhance their identities, express their own perspectives, appreciate differences, value other points of view, and practice fairness.

When children say "Let's pretend," they play together beyond their current developmental levels and social skills. Hunter and Ellison's clever strategy of using the dinosaurs as the characters in their drama helps them engage in tense negotiations and conflict. Their actions and conversation focus on who has more water, how to get more water, how to protect their water, and how to use the water together. Can you see how the children are using this drama to practice negotiating differences, exploring ideas about sharing and concepts related to equity?

Use the following questions to observe your group of children, looking through a lens of their social competencies and considering how they are growing relationships.

Questions for Reflection

How are children showing their approaches to working together? Are they interdependent? Independent? Dependent?

What do you see that shows what children already know about getting along?

How do children explore the sensory environment together, and how do these shared sensory experiences affect their interactions?

What do you notice about how children are moving together and how moving affects their interactions?

What repeated actions (schemas) do the children engage with together?

What dramatic play themes are they using to negotiate differences and practice fairness?

How do the children join in each other's play, inspire each other, and add new ideas to expand their play as they work together around shared interests?

Use these same questions as you study the rest of the stories in this chapter.

The Language of Music

A bird does not sing because it has an answer. It sings because it has a song.
—Proverbial

Ms. LaTisha, the toddler teacher, shared the following story.

When crawling and toddling toward the outdoor playscape, the babies often are attracted to the environment along the way. On this day they were drawn to the enticements set out for everyone to explore in our parlor. Tommy went for a marker to use on the easel. Zola's and Callan's curiosity was piqued by the instruments as both aimed for the drums. Zola crawled to the bongos and pulled herself up to a sitting position so she could bang on them. Callan wanted to join in, so he sat next to her to pat on the bongos with her. Zola used strong nonverbal communication to let Callan know that she wasn't happy to give up the drum. He understood her feelings and picked up the rain sticks instead.

Just then Ms. LaTisha began singing "Old MacDonald Had a Band," one of the children's favorites. The children immediately recognized the song and enthusiastically joined in to make music together. They moved their bodies and instruments to the rhythm. Callan shook the rain stick. Zola rocked and patted the bongos, and Tommy chimed in, singing "Eeeee" when it came to the "E, I, E, I, O" lyrics, waving his marker to join his friends with the rhythm.

This moment was full of jubilation and spontaneity. It was also intentional that the musical instruments were offered in the gathering space of the parlor to create moments of shared experiences and expression. We value music and its role in our culture to share stories using a language that transcends spoken words. Music empowers babies to communicate with their bodies, using the vibrations, gestures, rhythms, and all that encompasses the language of music. The babies in this story had a shared recognition of the language of this song and used it to express themselves as they connected with one another. They all found their own way as they used the rhythm of the song to feel the camaraderie of joining together.

The Power of Movement

We are constantly revealing ourselves to each other through our movement; learning from and teaching each other without even trying.

—Wendy Whelan, American ballet dancer

This morning our toddler friends were freshly rested and had recently eaten; they were full of energy and ready to move through their day. To support them we put on some music.

We observed a lot of smiling faces, jumping, holding hands, wiggling, and mirroring one another's actions and dance moves. The children even invented a dance circle to enhance their shared desire to move. This was an exciting way for us all to bond, using our joyful, exuberant energy.

We want to continue to support children to build stronger relationships with one another by offering a variety of exciting possibilities to engage in the natural ways they are drawn to move together. As human beings, we naturally move around a lot without even noticing, waving our arms, clapping our hands, shaking our legs, wiggling our fingers, and nodding our heads. Movement is also a language we use to communicate, through physical interactions like dancing, hugging, and holding hands.

Movement is a vital way young children build brain pathways to understand themselves and the world around them. Toddlers move their bodies

even more than adults. They explore how their bodies naturally operate through trial and error, and they are also curious to discover how their movements can invite responses from other people. This process is especially evident when it comes to navigating their arms, legs, and fingers. We often see toddlers spontaneously joining together with movements like running back and forth, jumping and climbing, reaching up and down with their arms, and moving their fingers across different materials and parts of their bodies. One child begins to move and then others imitate the movements until they have all joined in. This is simply a part of how children learn and connect with one another. It is also astonishing to discover how the children negotiate their bodies in space, avoiding collisions with one another. The children have an innate ability to see themselves and one another's bodies and movements at the same time. Other animal species use these sensory/motor skills as well: birds fly easily in flocks, cattle move together in herds, and fish swim side by side in schools.

We bring these understandings to our daily planning by setting up provocations and activities that can safely support our friends' explorations in moving together while encouraging movement that matches their shared energy, like slow and quiet before naptime or loud and riotously joyful on the playground. Observe your own group of children. What do you notice about the ease and jubilation of children moving together?

The Joy of Puddles

in Just-
spring   when the world is mud-
luscious . . .
when the world is puddle-wonderful

—e. e. cummings, American poet

Our children spend a lot of time outdoors, in all types of weather. On rainy days, finding puddles on the natural playscape is always a big hit for the entire community. The collections of rainwater throughout one week were a glorious gift. The children played extensively and generated new stories to tell while experiencing the joy of rain. We delighted when one child offered, "I'm making a cupcake soup for you with nutcrackers inside and a salad."

Questions for Reflection

Study the photos here. Where do you most see the shared joy the children have for immersing themselves in the powerful properties of lots of water?

Do you notice the children's exuberance as they splash, stomp, kick, and ride bikes through the water to make big waves and ripples?

Can you see the details of their faces and bodies as they earnestly take up the work of investigating the nooks and crannies and puddles and streams?

Where are children joining together to find ways to contain and transport the water?

This jubilant experience can play a powerful role in growing children's relationships with one another, with adults, and with the natural world we share. The children see and celebrate their passionate bond with the water and one another as they play. Encouraging children's engagement will help their connections grow while offering the adults inspiration and hope as they see from the children's perspective of the world.

Yet this water play can bring up many conflicting values that we, as educators, must navigate within ourselves and with one another. Water is a valuable, sacred resource, and how we use it has many consequences. We can reflect on these ideas to think deeply about our values around this important work for the children.

- How can we honor water as a precious resource while still enjoying it? Water that comes from the sky may be the most conscientious way for us to offer it for children's play.

- The water play requires more cleanup by the adults, as we help wet, muddy children get dry and changed. Is the play experience worth the space and time it requires?
- Are deep puddles dangerous for the children? Or are they a valuable play experience despite some risks they may hold?
- Will the children's play with the water harm the gardens and landscape of the yard or damage the bikes and other materials?

Adults can invite children's compassion and eagerness to contribute by alerting them to the importance of water as a resource and the need to take care of the landscape as they play. The children may also be enthusiastic about helping clean up the mud and water. When we center our values of community, connection, and collaboration, we can grow a more nourishing and equitable world, finding new, joyous ways to live together.

A Busy Salon

Children have always learned and created places for themselves through play.

—Historian Donna R. Barnes

The children had been repeatedly pretending to operate a salon for a few weeks. Riley was often the manager of the salon, and she tasked the other children with recruiting clients to get their hair done. We were intrigued by this play because it engaged most of the children at some point during our outside time. We marveled at how much they knew about this world of a salon and its people and roles.

We watched as Riley did Rocky's hair and soaked his feet in the spa. She pretended to shampoo his hair and checked in several times, asking, "How do you feel?" We also noticed Nalu, Tommy, and Elliot joining the play, if only for a few minutes, to get their "hair done."

Today the friends were back at the salon, and Evelyn invited Ms. Bianca, saying, "Come on and get your hair done." Ms. Bianca suggested, "Can I just get my nails done?" Evelyn agreed, and Ms. Bianca joined the group in the salon. Riley asked, "What color do you want?" Ms. Bianca requested seafoam green. Riley asked Annie, her employee, to "Get the seafoam green." Riley proceeded to do Ms. Bianca's nails while Evelyn worked on Ms. Bianca's hair.

As the children worked, they noticed the different shades of her hair. Riley offered, "Oh look, here's some black in here." Evelyn noted, "Yeah, and she has goldish in the front."

Adults who observed the play wondered what drew all of the children in. Was it a shared life experience surrounding a salon? Did they feel satisfied that they were knowledgeable as they engaged in this real-world context?

The children easily took turns trying out the roles of customer, owner, and employee. They took up the important, meaningful work of offering comfort and care. We can see them practice thoughtful interactions through invitations, good manners, and responsive service as they check in with their "clients." We can also see how this play provides opportunities for the children to notice and appreciate differences in others. Supporting and extending play like this "salon" through our interactions, environment, and materials has many possibilities for deepening children's exploration of their identities and encouraging them to embrace the social skills necessary for a civil society.

Real Cooking

The babies were together on the playscape one sunny morning. Sitting near each other they began picking up, touching, rubbing, looking at, and investigating the natural loose parts and real kitchen tools we intentionally provided. The leaves, shells, and rocks had varied weights, and we saw the children handle them differently as they detected the differences. They used two hands to pick up the heavy objects and more careful fingers to manipulate the leaves.

Their keen interest in the pots, pans, and utensils was palpable as they earnestly used them to fill, dump, and stir the materials. Although the children didn't directly interact with each other, we could see they were watching each other attentively, seeming inspired to try out what they saw each other noticing and doing.

The sensory elements of the beautiful loose parts, with their varied size, weight, colors, and textures, invited the children's common desire to immerse themselves in the natural world. Repeated actions in the children's explorations were visible as we saw them enclosing, transporting, and transforming. Although it may not have looked like they were actively creating a "drama," we understood that they noticed and were inspired by each other's ideas and serious work. This play provided foundational practice that would allow these children to share ideas and play together throughout their childhood.

The children share the playscript of "cooking" because they all have experiences at home and in our program of seeing as well as using pots, pans, and utensils for what they know is meaningful work. Do you notice the intense interest in the children's expressions and body language? They relished the idea that they could use the real tools from the important work of cooking to feed the community. Their attentive engagement showed that they were drawn to the real objects and themes that reflected their lived experiences. These children brought rich knowledge to this shared moment on the playscape.

The Traditions of Childhood

Playing group games embodies our collective joy! Playing games together provides a great opportunity for children to practice their natural social skills and grow their relationships. This play often generates something new and never before thought of while also carrying the traditions and ideas from one generation to the next—like the legacy of hopscotch. How many generations of children have played hopscotch or ball?

Hopscotch and History

"My nana taught me to do one foot and then two feet and then one foot and then another. . . My daddy taught me how to do math."

Today on the playground, Ms. Jessica noticed Lynn throwing a rock on the sidewalk and then jumping to pick it up. She walked over and asked Lynn what game she was playing. Lynn responded, "I'm playing hopscotch. My mommy taught me how to play at home." Ms. Jessica offered, "This game has been around for a long time. I used to play it with my cousins and sisters, in the road in front of our house. We used a broken piece of glass to toss in the pattern of rectangles and squares instead of rocks."

Ms. Jessica drew a number hopscotch on the sidewalk and said, "Let's play!" Before they began to play, Lynn told Ms. Jessica that she had to throw the rock first and then jump to pick it up. When it was Lynn's turn, she jumped and counted the numbers in Spanish, saying, "Uno, dos, tres, cuatro, cinco, seis, siete, ocho, nueve, diez." Langston came over and asked Lynn if could he play, and they both began to jump and count the numbers. Langston counted the numbers in English as he jumped. When he got to ten and turned around, he counted backward.

ON
THE

Playing Ball

Cruz (four years old) and Callan (one year old) had developed a special connection and bond. Cruz, like many of his older peers, was intrigued by and eager to be in relationship with the infants. The infants, judging by the feelings they communicated through gestures and body language, seemed to share the interest. Cruz took part in a project with a group of older children to create a chandelier for the infant room. During that project, educators invited Cruz to study and create a portrait of Callan. From these encounters their relationship grew.

Cruz loved soccer, often playing with fierceness and skill on the playscape. One day when playing outside, Cruz noticed Callan sitting in the grass. Their hearts and minds seemed to meet up as Cruz slowly walked toward Callan and squatted next to him. He rolled the ball toward Callan and positioned himself close enough for Callan to successfully receive the ball. Then Callan held the ball up and rolled it back. They both laughed and found joy in this sweet exchange. It was powerful for us to witness the ways that Cruz understood and honored Callan's point of view.

Questions for Reflection

When have you seen children join together to play a game, either games they learned from their families or games they invented with other children?

What games do you remember playing as a child? Where did you learn them?

In what ways do you share games from your childhood with the children you work with? What shared games do you still love to play?

A Helping Hand

Giving the small moments in life to your children helps them grow into stronger men and women.

—Attributed to the Native American Fatherhood and Families Association

Children naturally want to contribute to the well-being of others and the community. When children help, they develop skills and competencies while growing their self-esteem and their sense of belonging. Our values at the Highlander School support this natural desire to help. We promote our values in our daily life through sharing, cooperation, harmony with nature, and respect for all beings.

Throughout human history children have been appreciated for helping in their family and kinship networks. Most Indigenous groups have long believed that children would not learn the skills or dispositions needed for the community to survive if they weren't given responsibilities early in their lives. In modern times children are less often asked to participate in the real work of the community, which undermines their natural desire to participate as well as their sense of belonging and helpfulness. Study the following stories reflecting children's desires to help and contribute.

Friends Helping Friends

Callan had been interested in trying to ride tricycles for some time. One day, we were surprised to see him balancing on the scooter in the bike area. We wondered whether he would take the scooter out. Would he try to stand and push it? Had he been learning by watching how other children used the scooter? Was he using the scooter because he enjoyed standing and walking so much, which was so new for him? How would he face the challenges of steering and navigating uneven terrain?

Callan chose to straddle the scooter and push it along while walking.

Porter, an older child, was watching and wanted to help. He tried to show Callan how to stand on the scooter and push with his feet, with limited success. Yet this offering from Porter seemed to help Callan persist.

Porter stayed close, continuing to observe when Callan might need more help. Callan got stuck several times as he made almost a full lap around the path. When he couldn't get onto the bridge or his wheel went off the path, he used words and cries and pulled and pushed or squatted down, trying to find a solution. Porter noticed and helped him so he could go on his way.

Gift Giving

To build on a natural desire to contribute, we offer children opportunities to create gifts to celebrate birthdays as well as to welcome new children to our school.

One day, the young toddlers and multiage children collaborated in fashioning a gift full of marks and symbols to welcome a new child to the school.

Here were the children's conversations as they worked:

Ellison: I made two rolly-polies [pill bugs]. I love her.

Cora B: I gave a heart to you so we are best friends ever. I love you forever, and you can come to my house whenever you want.

Cora J: I made a zoo and there's people walking in there!

Not only does this experience build the children's empathy and desire to help others, but it also encourages children to engage together in language and literacy skills. We don't think about language and literacy simply in terms of children's academic skills or future economic function. Our ancestors inspire us in how they used their bodies and the earth as a canvas to communicate their ideas and as a means of expression. We want language and literacy opportunities to offer children ways to be in relationship with one another and the world.

WELCOME

Growing Where We Are Planted

Food for us comes from our relatives, whether they have wings or fins or roots. That is how we consider food. Food has a culture. It has a history. It has a story. It has relationships.

—Ojibwe activist and environmentalist Winona LaDuke

In our community garden, the children care for the people in their lives, as well as for plants and animals in the natural world. Together the children participate in all aspects of the growing, harvesting, and preparation of food at the Highlander School, from okra to blueberries to collard greens.

Planting Okra

Okra was brought to the shores of North America through the African slave trade, as captives hid seeds in their braids to transport them to this unknown world. During National Farm to School Month, we celebrate everything okra, including its history. Our toddlers have taken the lead in collaboration with their teachers, planting the okra seeds and caring for the plants. At only two years old they already understand their agency and their ability to make things happen.

Okra Development
Okra Drawings
Monday
Aug. 23rd
5 days
Aug.26
Aug.30

We introduced okra seeds to the children and invited them to plant them. The children had been helping to clear the remains of our summer garden and prepare the soil for the fall. Children have an interest in the garden and often want to help pull weeds and harvest crops.

Lassiter dug the hole, and Sullivan put in the seed. Then Sullivan handed some seeds to Lassiter and Mei to put in the ground too. Planting the seeds and watching them grow gives the children a sense of responsibility and patience while supporting their social skills and building their disposition for taking care of the earth.

Teachers Ms. Nicole and Ms. Akou invited the families to share in the details of their work growing okra with the children. Here is the letter they wrote.

Dear Families,

As our year comes to a close, we invited the children to revisit their work in the garden. It has been fun to think back on all that we have done over the past few months. During this last week together, we reflected with the children, looking at a series of photos of our gardening experiences. It was beautiful to see the children's excitement and notice what they were drawn to while viewing images of themselves and their peers.

While we had less of an okra harvest than expected, the impact of the experience continues to warm our hearts as we watch, listen, and learn about the natural world through the children's eyes. Exploring the process from seed to fruit was well worth the six okra pods we harvested.

The growing season is over, but our exploration is not. In the kitchen we will begin to cook our way into the new school year. We look forward to being in the kitchen and preparing a traditional Togolese okra soup with Ms. Akou. We would like to invite you to join in the experience during the break with your own exploration of okra dishes at home. We invite you to engage in your own okra experiences and share words and photos of your time together with your family. We would also like to receive any okra recipes you have to share as we bridge the connection between school and home with your family traditions. We look forward to hearing from you.

Thank you, Ms. Nicole and Ms. Akou

Harvesting Blueberries

Our blueberry bushes have been a part of the Highlander School since we opened, and they have become an important aspect of our rituals as a shared community and culture. They also joyfully announce the coming of springtime. Before going out to harvest the blueberries, we research what ripe blueberries should look and feel like before picking them. We learn that a ripe berry should be soft, dark blue, and easy to pick. If you have to pull hard, the berry may not be ready yet.

Ellison: Look, Ms. Jessica, this one is dark blue.

Jace: I found one too. It's a tiny one.

Ellison: I have 1, 2, 3, 4, 5.

Jace: I have two.

Ellison: I'll get the bowl so we can put them in there. We found a lot of blueberries, Jace.

Jace: I see some more under here (bending down to pick the berries off the bottom of the bush).

Ms. Jessica: We have to see what dessert we're going to make with them.

Ellison: I want to make a blueberry cake.

Ms. Jessica: We have to wait until tomorrow to get the results of our winning dessert.

"What can we make with the blueberries?" We posed this question to the children during the morning gathering.

Beau: We can make cobbler.

Alice: Blueberry pie.

Francis: Blueberry smoothies and blueberry syrup.

Joni: Cake, muffins, and waffles.

Brooks: A milkshake.

Spencer: Blueberry-strawberry milkshake.

Hannah: Blueberry pie.

Ellison: Blueberry banana pie.

Ms. Rukia: We can make blueberry pancakes and blueberry jam.

The children came up with some wonderful ideas about what we could make with the blueberries. Since there were so many blueberries, we asked the children to choose five of their favorite desserts so the group could vote for which of them we would prepare.

As the children engage together in the full experience of growing, harvesting, sharing, and voting on their favorite family recipes to prepare, they are working together as a community, along with seamlessly learning skills and knowledge, such as math, literacy, graphing, and measurement of time.

Preparing Collard Greens

To honor our culture and history we celebrate Juneteenth. We invited the children to help us prepare the collard greens for our feast. When the children approached the table to assist us, they immediately started pulling the leaves off the stems and placed them in the bowl.

Beau: We're helping cook the collard greens, right, Brooks?

Brooks: Yeah! I help my daddy cook collard greens at home too.

Joni: My mommy cook greens at home, but I don't think they are this kind.

Hunter: I think these are plants.

Alice: They are collard greens.

Hunter: Are we going to eat them?

Alice: No, we have to cook them first.

Hunter: Are we going to eat today?

Alice: No, we are going to eat them tomorrow for Juneteenth.

Most early childhood educators understand that children learn through play. Often we are pressured to describe the academic and school readiness skills that children develop when playing. Yet when we observe closely, focusing on children's relationships in play, we come to understand the deeper, more detailed sources of their learning and well-being. We see that other living beings are the center of children's lives. When we recognize and value these natural ways, all of us are nourished and thrive.

Questions for Reflection

What do you notice about the children's interest in these experiences of planting, growing, harvesting, and preparing food?

How do these experiences help children develop relationships with one another and the natural world?

How does the children's engagement in all of these stories reflect Winona LaDuke's words about food, culture, and relationships?

6 Our Diverse Community and World

It is not our differences that divide us. It is our inability to recognize, accept and celebrate those differences.

—Writer and feminist activist Audre Lorde

We reside in a diverse and beautiful world, full of varied ways of living, speaking, communicating, identifying, sharing, knowing, and being in community with one another. Our experiences and histories, and those of our ancestors, shape the essence of who we are and contribute to our differing perspectives and cultural identities.

At a very early age, children uniquely notice and appreciate the differences in the world, and this helps them thrive. They enter this earth from the sacred womb. They use heightened senses in ways that many adults have unlearned, using their intuition to observe, construct knowledge, and make essential distinctions. Young children recognize and compare the unique qualities of other living beings and the natural world. They can distinguish their mother's smell from that of others, they are in tune with the language of sound, and they understand the individual ways that other children yearn to be consoled. Children see and notice physical differences in skin color, eye color, hair, and body shapes and sizes. When describing what the animals might need in the community garden, a child offered, "A house . . . I sleep in a big house and a mouse lives in a tiny house." Children show us over and over that they recognize the diversity among all living beings.

Our role as a beloved community of learners is to honor the uniqueness of each individual being and life-form and find joy in our differences as we strive to create pathways for new understandings and strengthen our interdependence. Just as a bee has a role to play in the balance of our ecosystem, our diverse ways of being play a crucial role in sustaining our world. We think of the school as a village full of relationships. It is in this diverse community, our ecosystem with families and teachers, that children thrive. The Highlander School believes we must foster children's view of themselves and others as an integral part of this earth, as members of the family of all living beings, including their immediate family and greater community.

Typically early childhood programs divide groups of children by age. Some states even require this. We embrace the diverse ages of the children and adults in our program and larger community, understanding that historically children were not raised segregated by age. Tribes, extended families, and kinships have always included elders, relatives, close friends, and neighbors of various ages, bringing diverse experiences and knowledge to the community.

At the Highlander School, we envision a place of fluidity of movement and ideas, where children interact with many others throughout the school day and they can experience diverse ways of being to create a continuous thread of joy. We recognize that children of varying ages desire to be in relationship with one another. We have intentionally created a flow

with pathways, glass doors, and windows that empower children and all of us to experience the essence of others, encountering, connecting, and making meaning together. We continually see older children pause at the doors of the infant room, peering in, noticing the differences, and seeking connection. The babies and toddlers always respond with eager attention.

Gifts for Infants

We want to respond to the older children's strong and unwavering desire to be connected to our youngest citizens, the infants and young toddlers. In this spirit, we desired to create opportunities for exchanges among the different age groups. It is our culture as educators to respond by observing, documenting, planning, and generating questions to guide us. To begin a project we wondered:

- How do children perceive the rights of younger children?
- How do they approach or initiate relationships with younger children?
- What internal moral codes are evident in their relationship with younger children?

The children collectively agreed to create a gift for all the babies currently in the infant room and also the ones yet to come. To facilitate the creation of this gift and expand the project work, we offered the older children time to play with the babies in small groups. Using the understandings they gained from their playtime, the older children made portraits of each child as an initial gift.

After, we asked the group to talk together about what they learned about the babies when they played and watched them and what they thought the babies deserved. We asked, "What are the rights of babies?"

Porter: To sleep!

Ana Flor: They have the right to milk.

Sadie: To have room.

Grace: To sleep.

Ian: To walk.

Malcolm Lee: He doesn't walk.

Cruz: To drink water.

Malcolm Jean: He has the right to crawl.

Ian: To sit down. What is he saying?

Chloe: A bottle.

The older children's comments offered insight into their thinking and ways they noticed differences in the development and rights of infants.

After the play, observations, and discussions, the children were unified in a mission to create a gift for the infant room. Their design was inspired by the room's chandelier. Their insights about the babies brought forth new ideas.

Caitlyn suggested adding Christmas lights.

Ms. Nicole O.: Why Christmas lights?

Caitlyn: It's not Christmas yet, but I want to do it for Christmas because babies like lights, and I want some pictures for the babies.

Porter: But they already have lights.

Porter suggested adding a clock.

Ms. Nicole O.: Why a clock?

Porter: Because they don't have a clock.

Caitlyn: A cuckoo cuckoo clock is too noisy.

Ms. Nicole O.: What do babies like?

Porter: They like putting things in their mouths, and they like noise like Callan. We can put beads. If we spin it [the chandelier] around for them, it will make music.

Joel: Rattles shake and babies like things that shake. What if you tap the two wires together? It would sound like swords or lights sabers clashing together.

Porter: And the beads.

Joel: Let's test.

We believe navigating different ideas is fundamental in a democracy, so during our small-group work we challenged the children to work collectively. The children were comfortable combining their ideas into one design for the chandelier. They first worked individually and then studied the drafts of their peers' ideas and began to insert the various ideas into one plan. Each child took their peers' concepts into consideration as they illustrated their individual chandeliers. In the process of creating the chandelier, they encountered challenges with the design that required them to move their bodies through the space and see the world from an infant's viewpoint. The children continued to share their ideas and drawings, before cooperatively fashioning a large and final plan.

The children's strong connection and empathy for their younger friends fueled their desire and resolve to cooperatively design and create the chandelier. Their gift embodied a desire to offer the magic of light, sound, and reflections of each infant's identity. Our school celebrates the way children appreciate differing perspectives and diversity. It is important for us to build a culture that honors the children's identity fully and views diversity as essential for constructing new understandings.

Family and Cultural Identity

Beloved community is formed not by the eradication of difference but by its affirmation, by each of us claiming the identities and cultural legacies that shape who we are and how we live in the world.

—Author and educator bell hooks

As children develop a strong identity, they are eager to share themselves and their family experiences with one another. They use these opportunities to deepen their feelings of self-worth and connection to their family, as well as strengthen their identity and sense of belonging as they see and are seen by others. They come to appreciate the differences they learn about other people's families.

Notice in the following stories how we offer the children opportunities to share themselves and their families as they grow connections with one another around these important aspects of their lives. Where do you hear the children demonstrating anti-bias goals?

"Isn't My Picture Beautiful?"

As four-year-old Eve was looking through the room's Family Book (a compilation of the children's stories and portraits of their families), she called out proudly, "Isn't my picture beautiful?" Several children eagerly came over, wanting to learn more about Eve and her family. Here's what she told them.

Eve: My family is gonna be under the rainbow. Well, about my daddy. He always lets me watch a video game, my kiddopia, even TV. He always lets me go to special places, and he makes me pizza. I like my mom really good. One day my mommy let me go to the Nick Jr. house. And well what's special about him, he comes to my house; sometimes he doesn't. Tendai [Eve's baby brother] likes when I play with him. And we roll around. And also, I like his hair and beautiful brown eyes.

What better outcome can we imagine than a child being proud and happy to share the love of her "beautiful family" as Eve joyfully announces in this moment? She offers details about each of her family members, showing love, tenderness, and pride in her brother's hair and beautiful brown eyes. Eve also includes a friend in her story, alerting us that her sense of connection moves beyond her immediate family. Eve is developing a positive self-, family, and cultural identity, which is critical to all areas of her healthy development, especially her ability to engage in life-affirming relationships with others.

Drawing on ideas from Indigenous cultures and the National Association for the Education of Young Children (NAEYC) anti-bias education goals, the teachers and children at the Highlander School regularly study and invite positive experiences around the similarities and differences of the children's self-identity and family identity.

One of the ways we do this is by offering a Family Wall at the entrance to the multiage classroom. This area includes a display of photos and drawings and a table with a Family Book, a notebook filled with more drawings and stories that the children offer about their families. Children spend a lot of time engaging together around the Family Wall. They often stop to add more drawings and talk with one another about their family life and celebrations. New family members are added as babies arrive.

The prominent Family Wall shows the importance we place on making the children and their families visible. We invite children to see themselves and one another in positive ways and have natural conversations as they share, notice, and appreciate one another's similarities and differences.

Countering Inequity

Many people think that children don't notice differences and believe that bringing up differences grows prejudice and racism. In fact, the opposite is true. Children begin to notice differences between themselves and other people when they are babies, and research shows that they begin to show a preference for people who look like them as early as three months of age. When we adults are uncomfortable with differences and don't talk about them as a normal part of our lives, then when children encounter differences they come to think that "there must be something wrong with me" or "there must be something wrong with them."

This discomfort harms Black and Brown children who are marginalized in the larger culture, where they don't see themselves represented and are often portrayed as less important members of the community. If we are to counter bias and inequity, it is critical to decenter the white dominant culture as the norm for children and our vast world. The stories in this chapter reflect how we take on these important ideas.

The children approached the array of cutout facial features with curiosity and delight. The teachers marveled at the way the children easily identified their own eyes, nose, and lips and those of their friends. "That's me!" Norah exclaimed. They held up the cards, laughing at the images, and rearranged them to create portraits of themselves and their friends. The invitation was so well received that Norah decided to complete a portrait of each child in the room.

This encounter among the children amplifies how they find satisfaction in seeing themselves in the community as well as how they observe and process differences. We have many stories that highlight children's innate competencies for building relationships, empathy, and love for all beings. Our world is full of this graciousness and compassion, as we have witnessed time and time again. We see this when communities root themselves in compassion and respect, when neighbors help one another, and when anyone serves others.

This is what we want to hold in our hearts, as our collective hopes and dreams for our world. Capitalism, which offers a one-size-fits-all approach to education and where divergency is treated with disdain, is not a model for how we want to live together. We recognize that we live in an adult world that has learned to disconnect from the divine love within and has engaged in horrific atrocities—African chattel slavery, Indigenous genocide, the Holocaust, and the unyielding wars that remain with us today. We are these same humans, capable of both unwavering love and heinous acts of hatred. It is not enough for programs and organizations to uphold

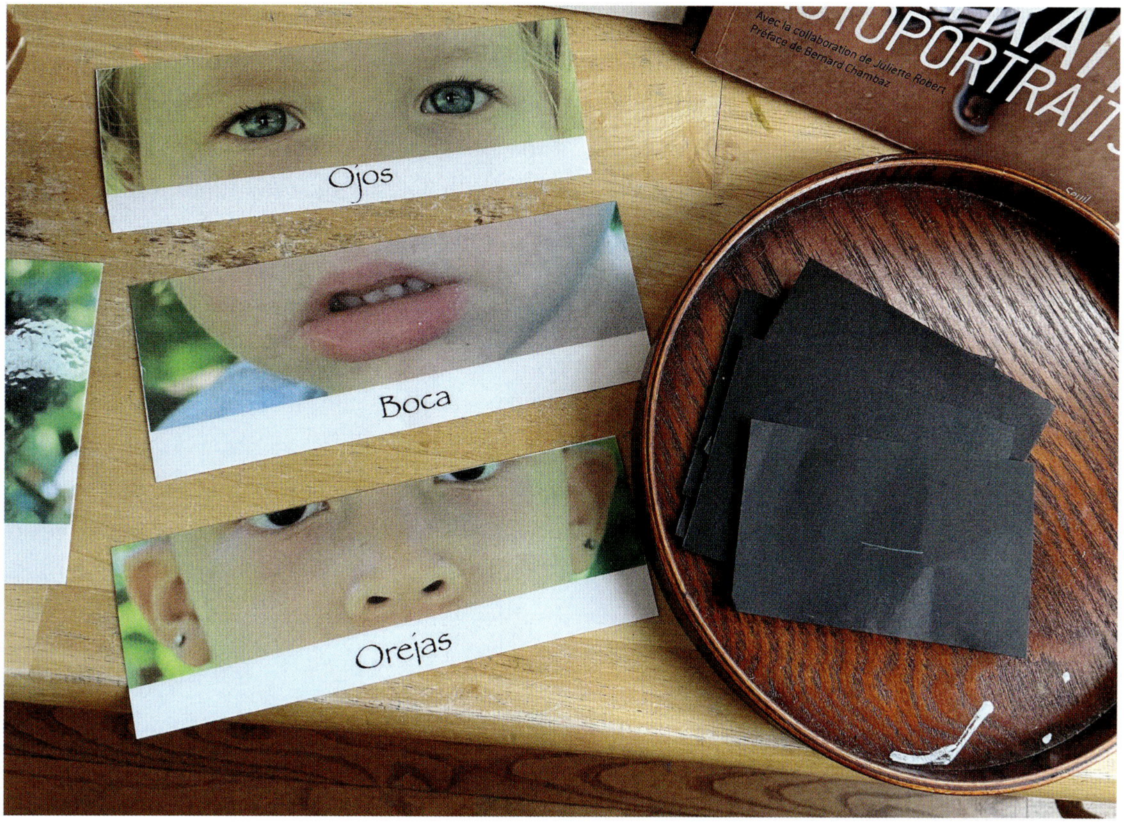
Ojos
Boca
Orejas

diversity and multiculturalism as a token value where we offer images of Black and Brown folks that reflect stereotypes. Reimagining the world and our work of creating a beloved community requires hard labors of love. We must have the fierceness to address systems and internalized beliefs that perpetuate racism, bias, and violence. Our work is to counter those narratives from a place of truth telling and love.

The pedagogy found in the schools of Reggio Emilia, Italy, that inspires us today arose from the horrors and devastation of World War II and survivors' commitment to developing an approach to education wherein dictatorship and fascism would never rise again. Our American history and this land hold similar memories of violence and trauma that as a culture we are collectively unable to address in our morality or our educational practices. With our work at the Highlander School we know we have much to learn from children about ways to navigate relationships, share resources, and solve conflict. We must resist messages and practices from the dominant society that are not designed to support a beloved community.

Pursuing anti-bias goals and anti-racist work supports us as we seek to live in this world together in peace. In our practices at the Highlander School, the anti-bias goals encompass more than just humans. Our hope and intent is that every child remains connected to this living earth; that they see themselves as an integral part of an interdependent, diverse world, where each life holds reverence; that they foster a sustainable earth for all to live and flourish; and that they have the courage to act and to resist oppression and harm in all forms and levels.

Love is justice.

Talking about Differences

By learning and talking about our similarities and differences, about actions to counter unfairness, we are providing children with a strong foundation to create a different world, one brave, heartfelt conversation at a time!

—Early childhood educator and author Nadia Jaboneta

We can support positive identity development and encourage appreciation and accurate language for differences if we notice and include experiences and conversations about the children and their families as a part of our everyday lives. As you read the following stories, see if you can identify more ways this can happen.

Our Beautiful Hair

The children noticed that the educators routinely wore their hair in different natural styles, including braids, Afros, and dreadlocks. The educators wanted to offer images and conversations that supported children with naturally curly hair to feel good about their identity and helped others recognize and celebrate hair differences. Teacher LaTisha offered photos of children with these diverse hairstyles for discussion.

Syrai examined an image of a child with an afro like hers.

Syrai: I like her unicorn shirt and her headband. She is beautiful. I like her glasses. I like her necklace.

Ms. LaTisha: What does her hair remind you of?

Syrai: When I have a fro.

Ms. LaTisha: What is a fro?

Syrai: Something when all of your hair is out.

Ms. LaTisha: Do you like wearing a fro?

Syrai: Um huh!

Ms. LaTisha: What do you like about your fro?

Syrai: Cause my mom gets to put it in puffs.

Noticing Differences

As Beau was revisiting the drawings and photos on the Family Wall, he named a discovery: "Hey look, Alice's dad is the color of me and Eve's dad is the color of Leland." Eve and Alice were playing across the room in the drama corner and heard Beau's comment. Eve held out her arms and said joyfully, "Yes, we have beautiful skin like our family."

Over his years at the Highlander School, Beau has been involved in many conversations about his skin color and that of his friends. This group of children have been together since they were babies and have been regularly offered ways to notice one another's similarities and differences. In the past Beau often said that he has brown skin. Was he repeating the words of his Brown friends to deepen his connections to them? Did his comment today reflect an "aha" moment, where he finally understands that skin color is related to his family? We want to continue to include experiences where children notice and describe their similarities and differences so we can keep seeing their perspectives and respond in ways that deepen all of our understandings.

Questions for Reflection

What is your comfort level when children notice and talk about differences?

How do you work to bring up differences and make them a typical part of your daily life with children?

Self-Portrait Work

At the beginning of the school year, children expressed interest in generating portraits of themselves, their friends, and members from our East Atlanta community. We coupled this emerging interest with the study of self-images and focused on the facial features such as the eyes, lips, and shape of one's head. We carefully examined ourselves in the mirror and found delight in our reflections. To support children's sense of identity and a positive self-image, we encouraged children to represent themselves using multiple mediums.

We began by exploring the power of drawing. As we drew, we invited children to focus on one part of their face at a time, first the eyes and then the lips. This allowed children to analyze in more depth the different components of those features. We began with the eyes, encouraging children to study the different features of their eyes and carefully draw them. The children used images of their eyes and looked into the mirror to create multiple drafts. We shared with the children language to describe the different parts that make up the eye: pupil, iris, sclera, eyelid, eyelashes, and tear duct. The teachers invited the children to look closely with questions like "How many circles do you see in your eye?" This helped the children focus on the details of their eyes, like the shape and colors of their iris. The process took a couple weeks.

Tommy: These are my eyes; I see white, and black.

Tommy was working quietly, constantly looking in the mirror, twisting his face all around and choosing many different browns to add to his paper.

As we proceeded to focus on our lips, we talked about how lips can be thick or thin. We asked the children to pay attention to the shape of their lips. Instead of drawing one line to represent their whole mouth, we encouraged children to look in the mirror and draw their top lip and bottom lip. Through this process we observed children becoming more aware and choosing to represent the small details of their faces.

Some noticed they had a mole, or several small freckles, or even a dimple when they smiled. These special and unique characteristics became a permanent part of their portraits. As educators we began to see the children celebrate these differences that make them who they are. We began this work with curiosity around how children would represent themselves and eventually saw them take pride in their representations.

Ami: I'm going to draw my bow in my hair.

Ansley: My hair will be pink because yesterday my hair had pink in it.

Annie: This was the shape of my head but I didn't like it so I erased it.

Ami: I drew my hair long because it's long. My lips are dark pink; what about yours?

Ansley: I made myself: I did a peach shirt and peach cheeks. I colored my lips with concealer, lip concealer.

Ansley was proud of everyone's work and mentioned how great it would be if we shared them and gave them to Dr. King. Annie explained that we couldn't because he wasn't alive.

The Identity Project: Exploring Skin Tones and Self-Portraits

We can disagree and still love each other unless your disagreement is rooted in my oppression and denial of my humanity and right to exist.

—Writer and civil rights activist James Baldwin

How do we create a society that affirms the humanity in all of us and our right to exist? James Baldwin's words are piercing and challenge the ways in which we approach our work with young children and address historical racism and discrimination. We began the school year with the collective zeal to take up brave conversations around race and identity and to continue to deepen our honoring of Dr. Martin Luther King Jr.'s work. We came to understand that diversity and multiculturalism alone were not enough to transform beliefs rooted in oppression but that new ways of teaching and learning were required.

This was made painfully evident by the teachers' observation of some children's preference for the white and light baby dolls even in a diverse

school community inspired by the work of civil rights activists. There were obvious disconnections. They decided to observe more and share their documentation with the families. Most of the white families concluded that their children selected baby dolls that mostly looked like them.

Christina, a Black mother, made a different statement, however, and proposed a question:

Christina: It is an interesting dynamic. It totally makes sense that the girls want to play with dolls that look like them. But I have to wonder, in a class that includes majority "tan" or "peachy" students (which may include mine from the Crayola perspective), what does it mean when the Black/ Brown doll is the one that repeatedly doesn't get selected for play? I wonder how that gets coded (and I am assuming it does)?

After a long pause, a white mother responded:

Heidi: I understand, as a white parent myself, how uncomfortable this topic can feel [for white parents] and how strong the urge is to avoid any shame that might come up for us. I appreciate that we have all chosen a school that is committed to anti-racism, as it speaks to our individual and family priorities. But sadly, we still live in a society that values white over Black. It is a hard fight to keep those messages at bay, and one I think

> requires constant vigilance and efforts to instill pro-Black messages. I agree with you all that it's probably natural for kids to want to play with dolls that look like them, but I think that it's our job to encourage them to move past that and to embrace more color options.

The exchanges between the parents highlighted the importance of offering the space and time to engage in challenging conversations to expand our understandings. Building on fifty years of research and increasing understanding of the pervasiveness of racial bias and internalized white supremacy, we reaffirmed our commitment to creating a sense of belonging for all. As a school, we began to lean into our anti-bias goals, inspired by and based on the anti-bias goals from NAEYC, as tools to support our practices and further our conversations as well as on our inspiration from educators from Reggio Emilia and Black and Brown radical activists. What does it mean to truly hold one's identity while valuing another?

www.naeyc.org/resources/pubs/yc/nov2019/understanding-anti-bias

If we are to support young children's full capacity to become optimistic, caring, social beings, we must work to strengthen their family and cultural identity and ensure we project visible, strong, positive images of the children and families in relation to the world around them.

The Highlander School Anti-bias Goals

Identity. Our hope and commitment is to support each child's self-awareness, confidence, family pride, and positive social/group identities.

Diversity. Our hope and commitment is to support each child's expression of comfort and joy with human and more than human diversity, accurate language or communication for human and more than human differences, and deep, caring human connections and connections with their diverse world.

Justice. Our hope and commitment is to support each's child recognition of unfairness (injustice), have language to describe unfairness or communicate their awareness of unfairness, and have understanding that unfairness hurts.

Activism. Our hope and commitment is to support each's child sense of empowerment and the skills to act, with others or alone, against prejudice and/or discriminatory actions.

Our slight changes to the original NAEYC anti-bias goals are based on our unique values, to honor the children's expansive inclusion of the more-than-human world as an integral part of our community and to recognize that nonverbal children are competent in communicating their beliefs with regard to unfairness and injustice.

In preparation for our long-term project on identity, we collected our observations, made meaning, and created intentional yet fluid projections on how to move forward. We worked in collaboration, centering our celebration and honoring of the work of Dr. King as a platform to discuss race and identity.

In our continued discussions about Dr. King, the children called attention to their own skin tones and the skin tones of their peers. Some children referred to race and others to skin tone. We noticed that our Black children were making distinctions between race and skin color but our white children were not doing this as often.

Sydney: I'm Black.

Beatrice (a white child): No you're not! You're brown.

Sydney: Yeah, but I'm Black American.

Beatrice: I have my daddy's olive skin.

Sydney: But an olive is green.

We were very curious about how the children conceptualized race. How were the children positioning themselves or seeing themselves when talking about the fight for civil rights? Was there a difference in how Black and white children understood what race is?

Our discussion with the children evolved into conversations about civil rights and some of the rights that Dr. King fought for, including the right for Black people to vote and the end of segregation. We also talked about the different ways that people protested for their civil rights, including sit-ins, boycotts, and marches. We continued to support them to have a better understanding of why these movements are important.

We believe that for children to engage in the third (recognizing unfairness) and fourth (acting to create change) NAEYC anti-bias curriculum goals, they must have an understanding of race and skin color.

To have a deeper understanding of the children's perspective and to partner with families, we sent home a family survey. We were curious about families' understanding around race and identity. In the survey, we asked how families identified themselves racially, if they discussed race at home, and how they described their skin tone.

We also looked for resources to support the children in having healthy conversations about skin color and came across Angélica Dass's photographic work, "Project Humanae." Her work focuses on "Humanity's true colors rather than the untrue labels 'white,' 'red,' 'black' and 'yellow' associated with race."

https://angelicadass.com/photography/humanae/

She photographed three thousand volunteers from their shoulders up and matched the background color to the skin tone of the subject's nose, then labeled the color using the Pantone color palette system. We printed out and laminated portraits from the project, then set them up around

the classroom along with Pantone paint cards of many different skin tone shades. The children examined them and talked about different skin tones. They matched the paint cards to their own and their friends' skin tones.

Our family survey and the comments from the children revealed that white children and families were not having conversations about race at home and had less language to describe their racial identity, culture, or power. Assimilation of Europeans and white supremacy stripped away Indigenous European cultural values. Ancient community-based, earth-centered practices, languages, and traditions have been lost and replaced with the normalization of whiteness. We recognized that white children needed language to describe themselves and to see differences as typical and valuable, to strengthen their compassion, and to promote their activism for fairness. Recognizing the privileges that come with white skin is necessary to challenge and change inequities and to stand against beliefs rooted in oppression. This is not about promoting white guilt but rather growing the children's understandings of how the larger systems maintain inequitable power structures that favor whiteness.

We then invited the children to create a collaborative piece with the children's self-portraits including their skin tone, and they embraced it. We wanted the children to walk away confidently and loving the skin that they had, while again celebrating and acknowledging the different skin tones around them.

Ms. LaTisha had transitioned into the role of atelierista, working with children and other teachers to experience and explore visual arts as a means of communication and expression. Her strengths were vital in supporting the school's many projects, and in this case she worked with all the children, pairing them in heterogenous groups and helping them mix their skin colors. We observed and took time to understand how the children represented themselves. We were intrigued when they stood firm about whether their color matched their skin or not.

Ms. LaTisha: What do you know about your skin color?

Ansley: Mines is peach and Evelyn.

Riley: Mines is black.

Ansley: Mines is this color (picks up white paint).

Riley: Like Beatrice.

Ansley: Yes, it's white.

Riley: Yes.

Ansley: Riley's color is the same as Ms. LaTisha and mines is the same as Beatrice.

Riley: Whoo it's turning different. I love black. Black make all different colors. It's turning in skin color.

As we worked closely with the children, studying their tones, undertones, and shades, we realized just how difficult it was to come up with language describing skin color. It seemed our lack of dialogue and practice acknowledging skin tones left little variation in the way people talk about skin color. From our white children we often heard either peachy or pinkish. We noted from our family surveys that some families struggled as well to come up with a description for their family members' skin color.

We wanted to give the children more language choices for descriptions and hopefully create a safe environment for them to talk about skin color. As educators we began to challenge our own thinking around the variation in skin color.

Sitting side by side, looking in the mirror with children and holding up the paint next to them to see the closeness in color, we began to really take notice of the variation. We learned and expanded our knowledge right alongside the children. At the end of our work, we invited the children to name their skin color. Several friends chose to use their own names to identify their skin color paint, or said, "I would call it 'Mine.'" We wondered whether a strong connection between the process of making their skin color and really studying it led them to giving their jar of skin color paint their own name.

Laylah: I see brown skin. I smile like my grandma. I like my brown skin; my sister has brown skin too.

Annie: I did red lips; this is my neck and dress and my hair is dark brown so I did light brown on the dark.

Langston: I see myself; my eyes are black.

Sydney: I put some other skin on my face because I wanted a little bit of different skin. This is my hair; my hair right here is tan. (She holds up the color pencils next to her hair in the mirror until she finds one she wants to use to represent her hair.)

Questions for Reflection

What is your response to the story about skin tones?

How comfortable are you in talking about these ideas with children and others?

How has your skin tone impacted your life and identity?

The following are some of the teachers' collective questions and reflections following this study. Ijumaa Jordan, a consultant, has worked with the school for years deepening and challenging our anti-bias practices. She led the following reflection.

Ms. Estefhaney: My research had shown me that children recognize racial differences at very young ages. Race is a social construct mostly used to categorize and keep people out of certain spaces. The challenge was how to communicate what race is with three- to five-year-olds, given that they were already aware of skin tone differences. Our Black children made a distinction between race and skin color, and our white children weren't doing that. They would say their skin color was "peachy white" or "olive," but Sydney would say her skin is brown and she is Black. Our Black children said "Harper is Black," and white children said "Harper is white."

Ms. Ijumaa: What did you learn so far about how children develop a racial identity? Why is there a difference between white children and children of color?

Ms. Tori: Black parents don't get to not talk about it. Your child is going to face it at some point down the line, so you need to instill a positive image of themselves. They are already being taught that lighter-skinned Black children are pitted against darker-skinned Black children. We live in white-privileged America. White parents don't have to worry about it; they are not facing the same dilemmas. If their child doesn't come back, it's because of an accident, not because of police brutality.

Ms. Rukia: What I learned was we have to do some things a little bit different with our work with our families when our children are younger. We have families coming here for the philosophy of the school. Parents aren't sure they'll say the right thing; they are uncomfortable.

Ms. LaTisha: Parents are worried about how another parent will react. White families are not fluent in it the way that we are. When your preschool teacher asks you this as part of a thread, you don't know how to talk about it.

Ms. Kendra: With the anti-bias education goals three and four, there needs to be partnership with families having these conversations at home in order for them to call out their own privilege and where injustice is being done. We have to do more work with our white children and our white families in regard to those goals; our white families are not having as much conversation about race.

Ms. Rukia: There has been a level of discomfort among teachers in the past. This year we have the most comfort; we had a lot of Black educators trying to "save" the white families from discomfort, not make them uncomfortable. Maybe because of professional development with Ijumaa, and we've been sharing more with families. We've had some pushback, and this is because it hasn't been mobilized as part of our culture.

Ms. Estefhaney: Ms. Bianca and I wanted to be a community of learners; hear from the parents. We are all trying to learn from each other and make meaning. Over time, we've become more comfortable talking about race.

Telling More Stories

Storytelling has become a fluid tool to celebrate diversity, offer counter-narratives, and center voices or perspectives that may be missing from our school. Our community as well as Greater Atlanta has shifted in demographics, losing many of the working-class Black families and being displaced by affluent families, predominantly white. Without intentional disruption by educators, children can develop assumptions and bias about their world when they lack varying perspectives. Books and stories are carefully selected and shared so the Highlander School educators can draw on the beautiful narratives of other members of our larger community. Not everyone has a car or lives in a house. What are the stories of water protectors? What are the stories of the people who help farm and pick our fruits and vegetables?

Acts of Love

We invited a small group of children to talk about the book *Last Stop on Market Street* by Matt De La Peña, as it holds many opportunities for children to consider different perspectives. It wasn't the first time we read this book, but the teachers wanted to get a better insight into what the children were understanding about the story. They wondered if the children knew what the last stop on Market Street was. Did they know what a soup kitchen is, and who eats at a soup kitchen?

Before we read the book, the children shared a little about what they remembered. Tommy remembered there was a little boy. Ellie said there was a grandma, and Harper said they got on a bus. Violet remembered they were going to Market Street. They knew there were other people on the bus, "Like the man that had the guitar," said Ellie.

As we read, Violet realized that the last stop on Market Street was the soup kitchen. Violet said, "That's where they make soup." We asked them who eats at soup kitchens, and Violet said, "Everybody does." We continued reading the story. Later we shared that a soup kitchen is a place where food is offered to people who are hungry or unhoused.

Ms. Tori: Why do you think they are homeless?

Violet: I don't know.

Ms. Tori: What makes them not have a home?

Violet: Because nobody build a home for them.

Tommy: Construction can build a home for them.

Ms. Tori: Well how can we show people that don't have homes love?

Violet: We can bring them to our home.

Ms. Tori: What acts of love did Nana and CJ show to the people around them?

Tommy: They went to kitchen. They went to go serve food.

Violet: I show love to my momma at nighttime; when I was about to go to school I gave mom a kiss.

Tommy: If we don't share food with them they will be hungry and if we share food with them they wouldn't be hungry and ask for food.

Ms Tori shared a story about an act of love she did on Sunday. She said that she was walking to get food on Sunday when a man who was homeless asked her for some money. She didn't have any cash but offered to buy him food and brought him some on her way home.

Tommy: That put love in his love bucket.

Ms. Tori: That was showing him love even though I didn't know him.

The teacher offered Tommy and Violet some drawing tools to draw how Nana and CJ showed love.

Tommy: This is them in the soup kitchen. Here is stove and food.

Violet: This is CJ and Nana; they are making pasta for stove and the food.

Women's History

At the Highlander School we are constantly considering what stories we will share and whose voices are missing. After some reflection, we realized that many of the heroes commonly shared with children are men, and we want to intentionally include more stories of activists who are women.

Moving into March, Women's History Month, we highlighted powerful and important women, including historical figures such as Susan B. Anthony, Rosa Parks, and Harriet Tubman, as well as women who are currently fighting for equality and change, including Malala Yousafzai, Michelle Obama, and Misty Copeland. We connected the topics of gender inequality and stereotypes with some of the issues the women were—and are—fighting against.

At this same time, we read *Goodnight Stories for Rebel Girls* by Elena Favilli and Francesca Cavallo. This book features many of the influential women we had already talked about and new ones we wanted to introduce. We used this book as a fun way of revisiting with the children. During lunchtime or before going outside, we played a game. We read a short story from the book but left out the name of the person so the children could guess who the story was about. We would also ask the children what specific issue (gender inequality, racism, stereotypes, and so on) was discussed in the story.

As part of our culture of supporting our community of learners, we asked the families and their children to share about a woman in honor of Women's History Month. We educators learned about some women for the first time, like Eufrosina Cruz Mendoza and Lucretia Mott. We extended our Women's History Month work by connecting it with our self-portraits, offering images of the women we talked about and inviting the children to draw their own portraits of these women.

We Want to Help Everyone

One day Rukia casually walked into the multiage room and noticed Ellie and Scout sitting at a table with a book about Dr. King positioned in front of them. They both seemed to be in deep thought.

Ellie: You know, Dr. King wanted to help Black people. . . . Well actually he wanted to help everyone.

Rukia was struck by her comment.

Ms. Rukia: What does that mean to you?

Ellie: That means . . . well I'm white and if I see someone doing something to hurt a Black person, I need to say STOP IT!

Scout: Yes!

Ellie and Scout both stood and put their hands firmly in front of them and in unison stated: "Yeah! Stop it!"

How does this exchange between Ellie and Scout help you to see the relationship between the ideas of fairness, equality, and equity? This exchange is at the heart of the possibilities of the Highlander School's work. This work doesn't cause white children to feel shame because they are white. They have experiences that normalize differences as they gain language to describe themselves and others. They also grow a deep understanding of unfairness and strengthen their courage to act. Courage is what this world needs.

Questions for Reflection

What are your understandings and experiences of unfairness in the world?

How can you strengthen your own courage to act, starting with children's certainty about the importance of fairness?

7 Fighting for the Beloved Community

But the end is reconciliation; the end is redemption; the end is the creation of the beloved community. It is this type of spirit and this type of love that can transform opposers into friends. The type of love that I stress here is not eros, a sort of esthetic or romantic love; not philia, a sort of reciprocal love between personal friends; but it is agape which is understanding goodwill for all men. . . . This is the love that may well be the salvation of our civilization.

—Dr. Martin Luther King Jr.

The two beautiful humans in the photo to the left have a special bond. They are the youngest and oldest in our infant room, forever engaged in a reciprocal exchange of communication through touch, babbling, and gestures. The eldest, Romi, has always been attentive to the younger Lewis, responding to his cries with warmth and concern. Today, Romi lays her body next to Lewis, as though experiencing exhaustion and seeking comfort. Lewis seems to understand the request and responds by gently rubbing and caressing her head while balancing his own body. Romi closes her eyes as he continues the embrace and she rests her body. They remain together for some time, sharing the space and their energy.

This moment between Lewis and Romi reminds us of the "overflowing of love" that is possible. We see how young humans are far from egocentric. They deeply care for each other and are eager to be in relationship with each other, sharing an empathy that is the root of social justice. Children are born with a compassionate instinct, seeking the "beloved community" that Dr. King describes.

Inspired by the notion of the beloved community as offered in the ideas of Dr. King and the ways in which we see young children naturally strive for these connections, we were compelled to reexamine the essence of his life story.

Questions for Reflection

What is your response to this story of compassion?

When have you seen the ways in which infants are competent at building relationships and acting on behalf of caring for one another?

Reclaiming the Story of Dr. King

One has not only a legal but a moral responsibility to obey just laws. Conversely, one has a moral responsibility to disobey unjust laws.

—Dr. Martin Luther King Jr.

Dr. King's life and work is deeply connected to the identity of our community and our school. He was a native of Atlanta; his image, spirit, and energy envelope our city. It is in this community and context that a young Martin witnessed and experienced the injustice and inhumanity of racism, while simultaneously his community helped him become the charismatic leader we remember.

We have celebrated Dr. King's birthday with enthusiasm and joy since the Highlander School's doors first opened. Our initial celebrations were filled with storytelling, preparing friendship soup, listening to and making music, and dancing. While these moments were fun and electric, they lacked the depth and fullness of his life story. A startling moment in our program sparked this realization.

Rukia's grandmother entered the multiage room with Stan, a family friend. Stan is a tall man of African descent with a prominent physique. The children were in the process of drawing and creating gifts but immediately paused upon Stan's arrival. The children's excited reaction startled us!

The children collectively chanted: Martin! Martin. It's Martin.

Luminous: Dr. Martin Luther King Jr. . . . We've been waiting for you!

Quynn: Dr. King! Dr. King!

Stan was stunned (as we all were), and he laughed out loud.

Luminous stated with such passion: Dr. King, don't go. We made things for you.

Stan with his hand held onto his heart stated: I'm sorry kids, I'm so honored, but I'm not Dr. Martin Luther King Jr.

There was a pause as the children looked bewildered.

Quynn gently asked: Well if you aren't Dr. King . . . are you Jesus?

In that moment we realized that we hadn't shared the fullness of Dr. King's story with the children. We had avoided explaining that Dr. King wasn't alive and that he had been assassinated. For the upcoming week, when taking our community walks, the children searched for Dr. King. Upon seeing posters of Black men, Quynn approached and asked with wonderment, "Is that Dr. King?"

Quynn's and the children's search for the real, living Dr. King became a metaphor for our own search to understand his life more fully. Unfortunately, we had offered the children a very whitewashed version of his life and failed to see their incredible capabilities to navigate this complex subject and process the subject of death.

As writer Matthew John reminds us, "The truth is that Dr. Martin Luther King, Jr. was an uncompromising social justice warrior and a left-wing radical who defied the liberal establishment, abhorred military conquest, denounced capitalist exploitation, and gave his life to dismantle white supremacy."

As a community of educators we began to ask ourselves hard questions. Who *was* Dr. Martin Luther King Jr.?

This resulted in a shift in our messages and practices of honoring and celebrating Dr. King's life and work with our children. We wanted to emphasize that Dr. King was part of a movement that included countless others.

We introduced the children to activists throughout the school year, beginning in our youngest rooms. Young toddlers became so familiar with the image of Dr. King and his story that they began to include him in their representations of their families. They saw him as a part of our community.

We also addressed the civil rights movement's fight to end discrimination against Black people and the incredible personal toll it took on Dr. King and so many others. Our celebrations included the joy, music, dancing, and warmth of our community's rich legacy, as well as brave conversations about violent police actions toward civil rights activists.

Honoring Dr. King has to include truth telling and supporting the children's ability to recognize unfairness and discrimination, while cultivating their compassion and confidence to act against injustice. The children have come to understand the deeper story of Dr. King's life and work.

As our older toddlers developed language around their racial identity and formulated more questions for the adult world, the teachers reintroduced the story of Dr. King and his good work. Holding a fresh image of children, we approached the conversations differently and did not omit some of harm he experienced, including that he was dead and he was murdered. The children became curious about how he died.

Ellie: What happened to him?

Ms. Tori: Someone shot him.

Syrai: We gotta take him to the hospital.

Ellie: Then the doctor can fix him. He will be alive; then he will fight!

Ms. Tori: Someone did take him to the hospital, but it was too late.

Vivian: His family is going to be sad.

Syrai: His children will be sad.

The children made drawings to reflect their stories. As we read the children's statements, shown below, we were reminded how children use languages such as drawing to make meaning of information and express their inner thoughts.

"The police put him in jail. I want to draw him in jail. I'm going to draw his kids. His kids are sad he is in jail."—Ellie, age two and a half

"The police is taking Martin Luther King to jail. Why is he so mean?" —Arla, age two

"He don't want to fight. He want to be peace. He is on rocks. He has to fight on there."—Violet, age two

"This is freedom, that's the sign. This is the letters. I'm going to draw him going to the airplane."—Syrai, age two

"He's never going to be a daddy again, that's why he is sad. He is checking his heartbeat because he died."—Ellie, age two and a half

"He is marching. His sign says Equal Rights."—Syrai, age two

"I draw MLK. MLK is happy! MLK fight. He fight for his baby."—Owen, age two

The children held deep compassion for Dr. King and his family, expressing concern about both his physical and emotional well-being. These brave conversations also added complexity and challenged the ways in which we adults view how to talk with children about "community helpers" such as police officers. We can easily see how different communities can develop a negative view of government officials, such as police officers, who enforce unjust laws.

Questions for Reflection

What is your response to the Highlander School's story of their work with children about the life and work of Dr. King?

In what ways did the children's words reflect their ideas about empathy, compassion, and fairness?

What is your practice for bringing up these difficult concepts with children? Do you try to talk about them? Why or why not?

"It's a Bad Law": Fairness and Justice

We have been inspired by children's compassionate responses when we explore issues of fairness and injustice. We want to continue cultivating our approaches to invite them into this complex work, having sensitivity to their responses and listening to their ideas and concerns while calling on their empathy and understanding of fairness and inviting them into activism.

On our community walks, the children expressed sentiments that food should be shared with all members of our community, especially those experiencing homelessness, such as Mr. Cedric. Mr. Cedric is a member of our community whom the children and educators noticed sleeping outside the library. When it was raining he would often sleep under the trucks. The children suggested that we share our lunches from the school with Mr. Cedric. The teachers informed them that they needed a special permit to share food from the school.

Here are the children's responses when discussing the law:

Seva: Maybe we can skip that.

Tommy: No! The police will come get you!

Dorothy: We need to have a fair law.

Harper: We need to give food to everybody.

Ms. Tori: What kind of law should it be?

Tommy: To show love.

Our dominant culture asserts that children are self-centered or selfish. Additionally, children are often groomed to operate from a place of scarcity, where we must be in perpetual competition for resources and materials. The children's words and beliefs, that needing a permit to share food is unfair and should be changed, offers a different lens and exemplifies children's internal understandings of fairness and sharing. Western research suggests that children do in fact have a strong understanding of fairness and most often choose to act to make things fairer for others as well as for themselves. Studies over the last ten years have shown that children are willing to sacrifice their own rewards to ensure someone else is getting their fair share.

The research also suggests that fairness doesn't need to be taught by adults and is not something that takes a long time to develop. Children naturally bring a strong sense of fairness for themselves and they are just as willing to stand up for others. Fairness seems to be central to developing understandings about how the social world works. Children, already possessing an eagerness for relationships, use what they observe to guide their interactions and relationships from a very early age. Educators, though, must be conscious and reflective about the messages they communicate to create an environment in which fairness, empathy, and compassion flourish. Do we use language that only supports individualism? Are experiences and materials offered that support sharing, fairness, and negotiation?

The children's passion drove us to invite them to write letters to Atlanta's mayor to ask that she change the law to make the sharing of food easier.

Aria, age four, wrote:

Dear Mayor,

Could you change this law for us? It's a bad law that says you can't share food without a permit.

Love, Aria

Questions for Reflection

What is your response to the children's ideas about the fairness of the law?

When have you observed children show a strong sense of fairness for themselves?

When have you seen them stand up for others on behalf of fairness?

A Garden from the Children's Perspective

Can we reimagine the world as children do, in which basic human rights such as access to food have been attained and thus aid in the cultivation of the beloved community? A dominant and recurring thread of the children's thinking at the Highlander School is the notion that food from our garden (and in general) should be shared.

In upholding this beautiful and powerful image of children, we are eager to learn with them and learn from them, to challenge our thinking about the natural world and food equity. We want to continue to create a culture in which children are empowered to have agency in this world now and to grow into adults as citizens engaging in activism.

As referenced in chapter 2, in response to concerns about food insecurity, we began conversations with the children about planting a community garden. There had been long-term discussions among the adults about using the sun-kissed space in front of the school as our garden, and we wanted to hear the children's ideas.

We invited the children to have a "dialogue" with the community garden space by exploring it with their bodies and senses. In small groups, all of the children (infants through preschool) spent time in the space. We observed the children running, touching, and exploring the space with their whole bodies.

We value the children's perspective and their ideas, whether verbally or nonverbally communicated. We spend our time in relationship with children, observing their play, work, and ways of being in this world, to guide ourselves in understanding how to move forward with our work.

Our practice for studying children's ideas often involves taping the conversations we have and transcribing them. We study and collectively make meaning of those conversations. We honor the voice and dialect that each child offers. Without the careful study of children's words, actions, and ideas, adults can often misinterpret or project a perspective that children do not hold.

As Sonya Shoptaugh, the school's beloved consultant, reminds us, "Words have power, and when we alter them, we change the essence to fit our own convenience rather than honor the inherent voice that spoke them."

Listen to the following stories about our community garden.

Questions for Reflection

What ideas do you notice the children communicating and sharing?

How do you make meaning of the children's ideas found in conversations?

Our Invitation to the Children

What does it mean to have a community garden? What food do you think everyone should have? Here are some of the children's comments when we posed these questions:

Eve: To share the garden with everyone, people that don't have food and doesn't have what they want.

Joni: For people that do not have a house.

Ms. Rukia: What food do you think we should grow in the garden for everyone?

Eve: We should have cherries.

Joni: Oranges, peaches, lemons.

Eve: Lots of lemons, a lot of everything, blueberries.

Joni: Bell peppers, broccoli, tomatoes, cucumbers, pickles.

Eve: Pickles and a lot of pickles.

Joni: Did you write down eggplants?

Eve: Pears.

Joni: Green pears!

The excitement grew as we saw this work unfold in collaboration with our beloved community.

Our Community Farmer

As part of our practices, we engage with experts from our community, who offer insight as we construct new understandings. Farmer Tenisio, affectionately known as Farmer T., is a farmer-activist, DJ, and agricultural educator. He was generous in giving us a tour of one of his farms, sharing his unique knowledge of farming and the land and leading the installation of our community garden.

During our conversation about who is in our community, it was clear that the children consider Farmer T. to be a part of our community. We asked the children to name members of our community:

Wystan: Farmer T.

Sunny: He was working hard. He was getting all of those wood chips.

Who Is the Garden For?

As time passed, the children's engagement with the space continued and so did our conversations. We remained curious about the children's concept of a community garden, especially since the COVID-19 pandemic had affected our walks through the neighborhood, as field experiences were not permitted. We also wanted to have a greater understanding of the children's views about the rights of the natural world.

Here's another conversation that added to our understandings. Notice the approach Rukia used in her interactions. The questions generated for these conversations were directly related to our Declaration of Intent focused on the natural world and food equity and our observations of the children.

Ms. Rukia: Who is the community garden for?

Margot: Everybody!

Hunter: Everybody!

Jordyn: Everybody!!!!

Margot: Um, sure. It's for Hunter and Janie and Jordyn and me and Wyt Wyt and Cooper and Janie and Hunter, and Cora B.

Janie: You already, you already said Janie.

Margot: Oh yeah . . . and, um, Cora J.

Ms. Rukia: Cora J. . . . So I hear you saying the garden is for all the children inside the classroom, so that's everybody?

Hunter: And teachers?

Ms. Rukia: And teachers! So it's for the classroom, the children, and the adults and teachers?

Janie: Yeah.

Ms. Rukia: Who else is the garden for?

Hunter: Animals.

Janie: Animals.

Ms. Rukia: Animals.

Janie: Cats.

Hunter: Cars.

Ms. Rukia: And cars.

Janie: And people that that don't have homes.

Ms. Rukia: People that don't have homes?

Margot: And and, and all of the people, a lot of the people that do not have homes.

Ms. Rukia: So what do we need in the garden for the animals? Let's think about this . . . to feel welcomed.

Jordyn: Food!

Ms. Rukia: They need food to feel welcomed. What other ways can we welcome or what are the things that should be in the garden along with food?

Jordyn: Rabbits like carrots because they when they see a carrot they eat it.

Ms. Rukia: When they see it, they eat.

Hunter: Yeah, we need to make carrots.

Ms. Rukia: We need to make carrots.

Janie: Yeah, for the rabbits, because the rabbits are going to be hungry, hungry.

Ms. Rukia: OK.

Margot: Rabbits eat carrots.

Ms. Rukia: What else would the chicken like to have in the garden to feel comfortable?

Jordyn: A pillow!

Margot: A pillow!

Ms. Rukia: A pillow. . . . I'm very comfortable at home with a pillow. What else do you think we could have in the garden?

Margot: A pencil.

Ms. Rukia: A pillow and a pencil.

Jordyn: Even a blanket!

Ms. Rukia: Even a blanket.

Hunter: Even a bed.

Ms. Rukia: A bed. Is this bed for the chickens or the rabbits or for all the animals?

Hunter: It's for all the animals.

Jordyn: We can have a bed for all the animals.

Ellison: Have something like food, honey, and water and all the animals can eat in the community garden.

Jace: It's for everyone who needs water and food.

Margot: Now it's time to make a pillow and a pillow. OK? The pillow is right here . . . the pillow is going to be too big for all the animals to get in the bed. I'm making the bed big.

The layers of the children's collective thoughts, ideas, and drawings conveyed that a community garden is a place of nourishment for all beings, a place for sharing resources such as food and water, and a place of security and comfort. This was a powerful way of communicating their beliefs about the rights of the natural world and food equity. When we open our hearts and minds to the insight of children, we return to a place of fluidity, flexibility, and love.

Questions for Reflection

What did you notice about the nature of Rukia's questions and comments and the ways the children responded to her?

What do the children's words tell you about the children's ideas about the community garden?

Fairness and Activism

In the adult world we often struggle to negotiate resources, frequently causing great turmoil. When we observe children closely, with the lens of looking for their natural social gifts, we see they have innate aptitudes for sharing and fairness.

We witness this every day at the Highlander School because we are looking for it, and we want to help it grow. We see infants seamlessly sharing food and toddlers giving up a coveted toy. Yet children also often struggle with sharing, just as adults do. The following story reflects the many ways children navigate conflicts and take action on behalf of the community.

A Story of Picking Blackberries

In partnership with our arborist, the children planted blackberry bushes many years ago. We have watched them flourish, yielding lush berries each year. The children recently had a fierce debate about the picking of blackberries in the school's front yard and how and when they should be

consumed. Some children, typically our toddlers, picked the berries with their families in the afternoon for their individual consumption, leaving none for others. When other children went to pick berries on subsequent mornings, they would find that all the ripe berries had been harvested. During a morning meeting, they exclaimed, "That's not fair!"

They decided to come up with an agreement. Ms. Jessica asked whom the blackberries were for. Later they made a sign reflecting their collective decision: "For everyone . . . the birds, the squirrels, everyone." The children believed the berries should be harvested together and shared, so everyone could have some. Imagine that world!

This story showed us that the children are eager to participate in the decision-making process and take action on behalf of the whole community. We decided we wanted to offer the children many more opportunities for active participation, and the community garden seemed a perfect place because it was engaging the entire community.

Democracy in the Spring Garden

The educators in our toddler room skillfully engaged the children in a discussion about the lush possibilities for our spring garden. The children eagerly approached the table to study the seeds and various images of plants. They took up our provocation to see the potential of what we might grow. The children had a long time to study the seeds and images and to share their own and each other's preferences. After several days, the children used their name cards to select which seeds should be planted. Listen to the conversation their teacher Nicole had with the children.

Ms. Nicole: What do you think we can plant in the garden?

Norah: Carrot.

Avett: Broccoli.

Norah: I have carrot in my house. I grow broccoli. A little tiny piece.

Jac Jac: A carrot.

Ms. Nicole: We have tomato. But it is too cold for a tomato.

Norah: It is not too cold for the carrot!

Ms. Nicole: Mei, what do you think we can plant in our garden?

Mei: Broccoli.

EXPLORE
RADISH

Clark
Jac
Lassiter
Penelope
Ms. Nicole
Ms. Akou

Ms. Nicole: What do you eat in your house?

Mei: Broccoli.

Ms. Nicole: What do you like, CJ?

CJ: Peas.

Norah: Flowers.

We are inspired by the following Loris Malaguzzi quote and want to consider all the ways in which we call on children to be activists and engage in the decision-making process, in their own lives and in the life of our community.

We can never think of the child in the abstract. When we think about a child, when we pull out a child to look at, that child is already tightly connected and linked to a certain reality of the world—she has relationships and experiences. We cannot separate this child from a particular reality. She brings these experiences, feelings, and relationships into school with her.

—Educational philosopher and child's rights advocate Loris Malaguzzi

Notice Malaguzzi's words made visible in the following story of the children's deep attention for and connection to the community where they live.

Questions for Reflection

In what ways do children participate in decision-making processes in your program?

How do you support children to see themselves as active citizens?

What skills do citizens need in a democracy?

What specific fields of knowledge do you notice unfolding in this experience? Science? Math? Literacy?

Team Everyone

To build community requires vigilant awareness of the work we must continually do to undermine all the socialization that leads us to behave in ways that perpetuate domination.

—Author and educator bell hooks

We view the child as a competent citizen who has a desire to be connected and make change in the world around them. We believe that the child's perspective is an important part of our community. With the upcoming gubernatorial elections in Georgia, we wanted to include the children's voices, soliciting questions they had for the candidates and asking about their ideas for improving our community.

We regularly take walks in our neighborhood, getting to know the people on the streets and the businesses around us. As part of educators' professional development, we created questions to guide our deeper understandings about how to support this engagement with the wider community:

- How do children view community and define community?
- How would children change the community if given the chance?
- How do children use their voices to speak up for social justice?
- How might children build connections in the community, in order to build their sense of responsibility for community?

After developing these questions, we met with the children in a small group to propose the project. There was immediate excitement and enthusiasm. During this initial meeting the children chose the name "Team Everyone" to identify the group.

As part of the process of understanding the children's thinking, we returned to the community over and over for walks. During one of our many walks, we were approached by a member of the neighborhood who was asking for food. She shared with the children that she did not have a home. When we returned to the school, the children reflected on the experience.

Beatrice: It is not fair because we just have houses and they do not have houses.

Rocky: I was sad because I wanted them to have a house.

Sydney: It is not fair that she did not get food at first.

Ms. LaTisha: Why?

Sydney: Because I did not think that was very funny when she did not get food. And I think she should have a house, so she could sleep in a bed, a very comfy bed. I think Ms. Nicky should have a house so she could relax.

As the children continued to walk through the community and generate questions for the candidates, they gave us more insight into their view of community. When the children noticed a lifeless squirrel laying in the middle of the street, the adults kept moving, but the children paused out of respect and sadness for the life that had been.

When we invited the children to pose questions for the candidates, Stacey Abrams and Brian Kemp, they were steeped in their points of view and their unique ways of noticing the details of our community and concern for their world:

Why do you want to be the governor?

How will you fix the cracks in the sidewalks?

How will you fix the signs in East Atlanta?

Why do people throw trash on the ground?

Why are there murals?

Can you help squirrels learn how to not go through the road while people are driving?

Can you help the squirrel to be back alive again?

How can you go to the store to get homeless people some food?

How will you build two houses for the homeless?

How would you build a house for all the homeless?

We assisted the children in fashioning a book of their work, including their ideas, experiences, and drawings of our walks through the community, along with their questions. We then prepared ourselves for Election Day. The children created ballots and some volunteered to be poll watchers. We agreed that every child in the school would have a vote and that parents could help if the child could not write. Literacy was not required for participation, only humanness.

g Citizens
Drawings of Nicki

There was an air of excitement among the whole community. Children's faces beamed with pride as they instructed the adults how to vote at the Highlander School! They held agency and power in this space. Later, the multiage children counted the votes.

Almost all of the children voted for Stacey Abrams, and she won in a landslide at the school, although Jalle reported: "I voted for Brian Kemp because he is handsome." We believe the children were highly influenced by the perspectives of their families, as we did not share our personal preferences. Kemp won the election by very close margins and became the governor of the state of Georgia. The children learned that actions don't always yield the results you want.

What is clear to us is that the children believe their voices matter, and we believe that too. Through this exciting project, we lived into our beliefs about how our community can learn together and take action for fairness. Each child was able to see themselves as an essential part of the greater community. They engaged as caring citizens, taking notice and taking action on behalf of their beloved community.

Questions for Reflection

What is your response to the story of Team Everyone?

What seems to be the most important ideas the children had about what the candidates should do? What do you think may be influencing their ideas?

How do you see the work of Team Everyone as a way to help children become responsible members of a democracy?

The Memorial for Breonna Taylor and George Floyd

Our school and world were in the midst of unprecedented times. Protests were being held in response to the horrific deaths of George Floyd and Breonna Taylor while our world community confronted the COVID-19 pandemic. Our school, like many early childhood programs, was closed as these events were unfolding. Our future was uncertain, but we were firmly committed to anti-bias work and reimagining a better world, so we pressed forward. Just prior to our reopening in June 2020, the teachers began having strong, emotional conversations about the recent events. As we returned to work, we noticed that many of the children were aware of the troubling happenings in our world and had participated with their families in the local protests. We decided to engage together in a project to help us respond to these traumatic events, and we wanted to start with the children's perspectives.

The following questions guided us in our project:

- What do the children understand about the current state of affairs?
- What do the children understand about the protests?
- What do *rights* mean to children?
- How do children view their rights and the rights of others?
- How do we help the children make connections between their performative actions and activism?
- How do we negotiate difficult topics in a thoughtful way with the children?

In the tradition of our school's values and practices, Rukia sent a letter to the entire community and offered a framework for thinking, inviting them to continue to create a beloved community with us.

June 10, 2020

Dear Families,

The Highlander School is committed to anti-bias and anti-racist work. We believe this work is crucial in creating a more just community and society. The recent death and murder of George Floyd has sparked an international outrage and collective grief, and it has also created an opportunity for us to be firmly rooted in our love for each other and passion about creating a better world.

Teachers began having conversations about two weeks ago about the recent events, sharing strong emotions. Also, since our return we've noticed that many of the children are aware of what is happening in our world and have participated in recent protests with their families.

Some of the NAEYC anti-bias goals have guided teacher's conversations:

Justice: Each child "will increasingly recognize unfairness (injustice), have language to describe unfairness, and understand that unfairness hurts."

Activism: Each child "will demonstrate a sense of empowerment and the skills to act, with others or alone, against prejudice and/or discriminatory actions."

We want to hear the children's thoughts and create a safe space where we can have these brave conversations. One action the educators would like to take up includes creating a memorial for those that have "gone back to nature" in an untimely and unjust manner.

For the children in the Toddler Two and Multi Age Room this would include conversations asking the children: What do you know about the protests?

Details of what happened to George Floyd will be omitted from these conversations. Simple explanations will be offered, such as, "A police officer hurt a Black man named George Floyd, and he died. The protesters believe what happened was wrong."

We will share pictures of the dearly departed, describing them in ways that humanize their story. "George Floyd was a father. Breonna Taylor was a community helper and worked as an EMT."

We will invite the children to draw pictures of those who have passed away, very similar to our Day of the Dead celebrations.

We will reassure children that we as a community and especially their families will keep them safe.

We will use words and phrases to explain the events, such as *protests*, *unfairness*, *racism*, and *Black Lives Matter*.

Please continue to have these brave conversations at home and know that this is a process, and it will not be perfect for any of us. PLEASE continue to expose children to diversity in an authentic way. Don't just share books about Blacks, Latinx, Asian, or children of color in reference to racism and police brutally (which can reinforce stereotypes) but include books/materials/movies that normalize our existence. We are bird-watchers, geeks, skateboarders, doctors, foodies, and everything in between!

Resources: www.wbur.org/onpoint/2020/06/02/teach-talk-children-racism-violence-protests-race?

With the Kindest Regards,

Rukia Rogers and The Highlander School Educators

We value transparency and recognize that relationships are the center of our work. This includes a culture of having brave conversations and creating an environment where challenging subjects can be addressed. We believe this invites others and our community to be thoughtful and reflective in considering different perspectives, being challenged, and constructing new understandings. We are also open about our practices and values, and we move forward with the assumption that others joining our community hold the same beliefs.

After sending the letter, we received responses from families:

Ms. Rukia,

We've been having a lot of conversations in our home lately about anti-racism, as you can imagine, and it has reminded me of how thankful I am for the difficult anti-racist work you are already doing at THS. From the way you have cultivated an anti-bias library to the holidays you choose to observe (MLK Day, Juneteenth) and the ways you advocate for your teachers, you are leading us parents and our children to do better and be better than white supremacy.

I also want to name the fact that I am a white woman who has personally benefited in 1,000,000 ways from white supremacy. I walk around in my privilege every day. I can look up and see the things that privilege has bought me. And I have not done enough to right the wrongs that have been done to you and your people both personally and systematically. I know I cannot "outsource" anti-bias work to THS, and I am ramping up efforts to support POC and specifically the Black community on my own. But I also wanted to let you know I am here for THS and you personally. Please let me know your needs as they arise and how my family can support your work.

One final thing, and I deeply hope this is not a triggering comment: I am very aware of the long history of Black women taking care of white women's children. And I am incredibly grateful for the ways you've subverted that dynamic by bringing dignity and power to the role of the infant educator. I have enormous respect for you and the educators at THS. My daughter doesn't just have incredible role models in her life; she has incredible Black role models in her life. To her, a Black woman is someone who is intelligent, powerful, creative—someone who leads and challenges others. You made that happen.

—Parent

Hi Rukia,

Thank you for the heartfelt message. The past few weeks have shifted my perspective in a meaningful way. My religion is kindness but I realize that is not enough. Real change must happen for our world to be a good safe place for everyone. I am listening and will continue to do so with Luke and Beau. Actions are important, and I am dedicated to making a difference. I support you, the Highlander staff, and am thankful for your guidance.

—Parent

In reopening the school, we knew that many children had participated in protests, had watched the news, and had bits of information about recent events. We were curious about how the children were making meaning of their world. We were also challenged with the importance of having brave conversations with children and doing so in an appropriate way. We first met with the families of the children who would participate in the conversations to create the space and time to hear their voices, and then our conversations began with the children.

We asked the children, "What do you know about protests?"

We shared a photo of Scout protesting with her parents in Grant Park.

Scout, looking at the picture: That's me on my scooter with my mom, dad, and Rosie. I'm holding a sign.

Ms. Jessica: Can you tell us what your sign says that you are holding?

Scout: It says Black Lives Matter!

Ms. Jessica: Why do you think your mom, dad, and all the other people are protesting and shouting "Black Lives Matter"?

Scout: Black Lives Matter!

Laylah: Don't shoot.

Ms. Jessica: Many people are angry because the police officer hurt George Floyd and he died. Can you tell me what you know about George Floyd?

Scout: I know his skin is pretty. I like the way he shapes.

Laylah: His skin is brown like my skin and your skin. A lot of people are angry and sad about George Floyd.

Ms. Jessica: His skin is dark brown like our skin. Yesterday, we talked about George Floyd being a brother and father. He had two daughters and a son who are sad because their daddy went back to nature.

Laylah: He was hurt by the police and died. What happened to his daughter?

Ms. Jessica: She is home with her mom. Do you think it's fair for the police to hurt someone because of the color of their skin?

Scout: No.

Laylah: No.

Ms. Jessica: Police officers should treat all people the same regardless of their skin color. Do you remember Breonna Taylor? [Scout and Laylah say no.] She's the EMT who helps people.

Laylah: Grandma Khaleelah and Sherron helps people.

Ms. Jessica: Can you tell us something about what your Grandma Khaleelah does?

Laylah: Yes, she works at the hospital and she puts on the suit and she said everybody is coming in with the coronavirus.

Ms. Jessica: Do you know what happened to Breonna Taylor?

Laylah: Hmmm, no.

Scout: No.

Ms. Jessica: The police went into her house while she was sleeping. They hurt her and she died.

Laylah: Like my uncle Shahid!

Ms. Jessica: No, Laylah, not like your Uncle Shahid; he died in a car accident. It upsets us that Black and Brown people have been treated unfairly for a long time. Do you know that's called *racism*?

Laylah: Racism, what's racism?

Ms. Jessica: Racism is when people treat others unfairly because of the color of their skin. Breonna Taylor had the right to feel safe in her own home. George Floyd had a right to feel safe going to the store. I want to be able to go to the grocery store and go walking in my neighborhood and feel safe. Do you want to feel safe when you walk down the street or go to the store?

Laylah: I want to feel safe when I walk down the street even when people ride their bikes. I wanna feel safe.

Ms. Jessica: All the educators at THS and your parents are going to keep you safe.

Scout: How that happen?

Ms. Jessica: We are going to make sure you are treated fairly. That's why people are protesting to make sure these injustices don't continue to happen in our city, country, and world. We love all of you regardless of the color of your skin.

Laylah: I like my parents; they keep me safe.

Ms. Jessica: Yesterday, we discussed making a memorial for George Floyd and Breonna Taylor with Ms. Rukia.

Ms. Rukia: THS wants people to know that it's not fair either, so we want to make a space so that we can remember Black people and Brown people who were killed or hurt by the police. What do you think we can do?

Scout: We can hang the pictures around the classroom.

Ms. Jessica: Good idea, Scout!

Laylah, pointing to photos: We can hang one of these pictures in the other classrooms, that one in infants, that one in my mom's room, that one in Toddler One, and that one in my room. That will help us remember them.

Scout: Yeah! That will help us remember; that was my idea.

As usual, we offered the children another way besides words to express their ideas. We placed cut paper and thinking pens and photos of George Floyd and Breonna Taylor and asked the children if they would like to draw a picture of them. Here is a conversation that unfolded as they worked.

Harper: People are putting out signs because the police hurt George Floyd and Breonna Taylor. That's why we are making signs that says Black Lives Matter.

Ms. Jessica: What do you notice about Breonna's face?

Harper: She looks happy. I like her sparkle glittery eyeshadow. I like the color of her skin; it's light brown like mines.

Laylah: She looks excited. I like how her teeth are clean and I like her smile.

The children began creating gifts for Breonna Taylor and George Floyd, offering items that they loved and cherished.

Joni: I made Breonna Taylor a gift and George Floyd. A gift for her and the both of them because they are very, very special. And so she can be happy, because for Black people.

Eve: I drew a rainbow and a star and a unicorn because I wanted her to be happy. And this one, George Floyd and Breonna Taylor are holding hands. It's a design. We made it for George Floyd and Breonna Taylor. Well, me and Ellie did some rainbows. I did some hearts and I did some flowers.

Eleanor: Me and Eve drew the rainbow in the middle. Flowers on the side.

Additionally, we installed a mural honoring the lives of Breonna Taylor and George Floyd as a permanent feature on our building. The children added the final touches, showcasing their ideas and compassion. This space is also for us as a community to always remember that their lives mattered and our quest for a just world is ongoing. This quote from Carlina Rinaldi captures our passion and energy for this work with the children.

The child is not a citizen of the future; he [sic] is a citizen from the very first moment of life and also the most important citizen because he represents and brings the "possible" . . . a bearer, here and now of rights, of values, of culture. . . . It is our historical responsibility not only to affirm this but [to] create cultural, social, political and educational contexts which are able to receive children and dialogue with their potential for constructing human rights.

—Reggio Emilia educator Carlina Rinaldi

Finally, this profound quote from one of the children perfectly captured all of our work.

"I want them to know that they are loved."

Questions for Reflection

What is your response to the story of the Highlander School's work about the murders of George Floyd and Breonna Taylor?

What did you notice about the impact that what the children had been hearing about these events in their community had on their understandings of their world?

How did the children's experiences influence the Highlander School staff's approach to this work?

What thoughts, ideas, and feelings did the children's words and drawings reflect what they noticed and cared about?

What did you notice about the teacher's approach to the difficult conversations with the children?

How would you have thought about this in your own work?

Growing Our Sense of Place and Kinship with the Land

Being naturalized to place means to live as if this is the land that feeds you, as if these are the streams from which you drink, that build your body and fill your spirit. To become naturalized is to know that your ancestors lie in this ground. Here you will give your gifts and meet your responsibilities. To become naturalized is to live as if your children's future matters, to take care of the land as if our lives and the lives of all our relatives depend on it. Because they do.

—Robin Wall Kimmerer, *Braiding Sweetgrass*

We are a nature-centered school and recognize our interrelated roles in helping maintain a sustainable earth. This earth is not just for the consumption and enjoyment of humans. Instead, we consider nature from an African and Indigenous viewpoint that understands that this land, this earth, every tree, and every being holds a spiritual essence and has rights. Our ability to thrive is interconnected.

Our Highlander School community in Atlanta has been evolving as we rethink our relationship with the land upon which we live and the natural world. We find ourselves asking, "Who am I, who are we in relationship to this earth?" This current thinking and our ongoing work is being fueled by our careful attention to children's connection with this earth and is further propelled by an urgent call to help defend the Weelaunee Forest, also known as the South River Forest, in Atlanta.

The land we are on is the ancestral home of the Muscogee People, and upon their forced removal, it was cared for by enslaved Africans. To heal from past atrocities, we must acknowledge the history this land holds and the legacy of the physical and cultural genocide that took place here. We cannot do this work without centering the futurity, voices, and knowledge of African and Indigenous Americans and the voice of Earth herself.

The Weelaunee Forest is located less than five miles from our school, and these grounds are currently under threat of destruction and deforestation. The forest is targeted as a site for building a police militarization base known as "Cop City"; another significant portion of the land could be bulldozed for the construction of a Shadowbox Studios film-making facility. Community members have organized and collaborated with Muscogee People to stop the building projects in the forest. This has been part of the ongoing reconnection of Muscogee People to their ancestral land. Young children offer a unique perspective and kinship with the natural world that hasn't been subdued by capitalism's tendency to commoditize the gifts of this earth. For example, we witnessed the children's empathy for trees when planting them on our playscape. We asked, "What do the trees need to feel welcomed here at the Highlander School? What do the trees need to feel love here?" Let's revisit the conversation from chapter 3 about the children's empathy for trees when planting them on our playscape.

Hunter: Hugs.

Ellison: Hugs on the tree.

Jace: Medicine.

Cooper: And water.

Ellison: And sun.

Eve: We could give the trees lots of love and we could come out every day to check to see if it's here or not.

Margot: Water.

Ellison: Love . . . Good Stuff.

Eve: We could make a sign that says there are trees, there are fruit trees, there are a lot of stuff you could eat.

Margot: I can give them my lovie. We can make a small toy for the tree. We give them hugs and kisses; they will be happy.

We knew that the children held a deep love and appreciation for the trees in their immediate space, and we were confident that this affection would extend to the Weelaunee Forest if given the opportunity. With this assumption, our parent-led Social Justice Committee helped organize visits to the forest including educators, children, and families. The families recognized the importance of this forest, yearning for their children to be connected to it and, as a parent stated, to have the "belief that they can take action on issues that matter."

We explored the Weelaunee Forest, embracing her and knowing her. Children moved slowly through the space, experiencing the sensuality of the forest with their bodies. They stopped often, leaning into the earth in dialogue. Ms. Estefhaney shared the ways in which the land told stories we could hear when we slowed down to listen, the stories of the water puddles, the baby oak tree, the pine cones, the caterpillars, the sticks, and pine needles.

As educators we returned to the questions and inquiries in our Declaration of Intent. We wondered:

- What does it mean to be in relationship with the land we inhabit?
- How do children view the rights of the natural world?
- How do children show us and communicate with us their deep yearning to be in relationship with others and the world around them?
- What can we learn from children about how they connect, perceive, and relate to the natural world?

Later, we invited families to have conversations with children about their encounters. Inside the school we wanted to create a context for the children to continue their conversations and share what they noticed, explored, and learned with children who did not go to the forest. We used the parlor inside our building entry to create a digital landscape. Educators Estefhaney, Daisey, and Latisha leaned into rigorous thought about how to bring the Weelaunee Forest into our space. We played videos from our walks, printed images of the children in the forest, and incorporated the gifts of natural materials we collected from the forest. We wanted to create a space and the time for children to revisit and reconnect with the Weelaunee Forest, as well as to honor it. The children immediately began to share stories with one another.

Parent Reflection from Weelaunee Forest

As we walked through the forest, Lassiter wanted to stop and look at every last tiny detail. It forced me, a lifelong "indoors kid," to slow down and closely examine the plants and creatures I would otherwise have passed by. I think our kids can sometimes force us into mindfulness that way. I commented that the trees seemed young, and one of the forest defenders explained that the land was cleared for plantations by enslaved people and has only "recently" grown back. So many of the trees were only about sixty years old. I was struck by how long and painstaking a process it is to grow a forest. And how easily it can be undone.

Coming from a capitalistic, colonizing culture, it's easy for me to feel disconnected from the natural world. Like all of us, I try to buy less, walk more, use less plastic, compost, etc. But thinking about "the rights of the natural world" reframes conversations about climate change in an interesting way. Who told us we had the right to take things from the earth? When did we decide the earth belonged to the people with enough power to take it?

I always assumed climate change was a separate and distinct issue from that of racial justice. But learning about the multilayered history of the Weelaunee Forest (first taken from the Muscogee People, then cleared and farmed by enslaved people, and now set aside for a massive police training center), it's becoming clear how interconnected they are. And it makes me wonder what other important details I am missing as I pass by.

—Mother of Lassiter (age three)

After multiple visits to the Weelaunee Forest, we decided that it was time to offer the children some of the land's history, the immediate plans to cut down the trees, and the return of the Muscogee People to protect it. We created a short story that spoke to the forced removal of the Muscogee People from their home and their return back home. Hunter continuously interrupted and asked, "Why? Why did the white people do that? Why do they want to cut down the trees?"

The question "why" at times was challenging to answer but upon reflection Hunter shed light on the necessity of challenging narratives and the need to demand reasons for people's actions. When we shared that the Muscogee children were returning to their homelands in efforts to protect the Weelaunee Forest, Hunter exclaimed, "Is this for real? They are really coming!" The children cheered with excitement but soon this enthusiasm turned to dismay as we shared the plans to cut down the trees.

In response, Jace placed his hand over his heart, turning to friends in disbelief.

Cora B: Do the people know? We need to tell all the people in the town! We need to tell the people!

Ms. Estefhaney: What would we tell the people?

Ellison: Stop it!!

Cora B: Don't cut down the trees!

Ms. Rukia: How will we tell the people?

Cora B: We'll shout it!

Maverick: We can write it down.

Jace: I know: we can write it on each tree.

We began to support the children's ideas both to create signs and to tell the people. Much time was spent pondering the tree's perspective. What do you believe the trees want to communicate? What would they want the signs to say?

Cora B: He is trying to say don't cut the tree down because we don't want the trees to get pushed down. We want to save them. We got to save the trees!

Ellison: They can't talk. Maybe if we had magical dust glitter and then the glitter can make them talk? Maybe that can work.

Cora B: Don't knock down the rest of the trees.

Building from their understanding and perspective, the children began to create signs on behalf of trees, speaking to and for them. Their language was fierce, strong in ways that they did not usually express on behalf of themselves. This ongoing project has truly been a reciprocal learning process for us all. It is powerful to witness and feel the children's passion and sense of agency to act on behalf of their community and in solidarity with other children, families, activists, Indigenous people, and educators. Children embody such sensitivity to this earth and a belief in the right of trees to existence, to hugs, to love, to happiness, to the sun, to water, to a lovie, to medicine, and to the good stuff! Our adult world has a good deal to learn from children about empathy and its expansiveness to be bestowed on all beings.

In the days to follow, the conversations continued and the children's emotions grew. The children continuously talked about the trees and the Muscogee People returning. The stories about the Weelaunee Forest and

the Muscogee People began to flow in their play and interactions. The children were also invited to make gifts for the guest speakers of the Muscogee summit organized by the broader community.

Mekko Chebon Kernell, a leader among the Muscogee community in Oklahoma, said, "Georgia's school system speaks of the Muscogee People as though we are from the past. We want folks to know that we are still here fighting for this earth, land, and water." Chebon Kernell's message resonated with our hearts and minds as we recognize our interrelated roles in creating harmony and balance with this earth.

In this spirit of sharing with others what was occurring in the Weelaunee Forest, our children invited children from other preschool programs to join them in the forest. As this work progressed, the invitation to join resulted in children across five preschools in the area rallying for a child-led protest throughout the East Atlanta Village.

The words of two leaders sum up the essence of this experience. Dr. Laura Harjo, a Muscogee scholar, was brought to tears hearing of the children's conversations, saying, "This was the children forming kinship relationships with me and my ancestors."

And Loris Malaguzzi reminds us: “We can never think of the child in the abstract. When we think about a child, when we pull out a child to look at, that child is already tightly connected and linked to a certain reality of the world—she has relationships and experiences. We cannot separate this child from a particular reality. She brings these experiences, feelings, and relationships into school with her.”

Our story is far from over, but we’ve come to the end of this book. The Highlander School is now ten years old, and our stories continue to grow. What would it mean for you to look at your own life and work through the lens of the stories in this book?

For you, the reader, we hope this is the beginning of an expanded journey to put to good use your investment of time, your reflections, the questions you have uncovered for yourself, and the courage that has been called out in you.

Consider your aspirations for this journey. Consider developing your own Declaration of Intent to guide you on shaping your own work into a beloved community that experiences joy even as you do the hard work of bringing your aspirations to life.

Index